ZEN

AND THE ART OF
ANYTHING

BROADWAY BOOKS

NEW YORK

Zen

AND THE ART OF
ANYTHING

HAL W. FRENCH

Illustrations by Marianne Rankin

A hardcover edition of this book was originally published in 1999 by Summerhouse Press.

ZEN AND THE ART OF ANYTHING. Copyright © 1999 by Hal French, Illustrations copyright © 2001 by Marianne Rankin. All rights reserved. Printed in the United States of America. No part of this book may be reproduced or transmitted in any form or by any means, electronic or mechanical, including photocopying, recording, or by any information storage and retrieval system, without written permission from the publisher. For information, address: Broadway Books, 1540 Broadway, New York, NY 10036.

Broadway Books titles may be purchased for business or promotional use or for special sales. For information, please write to: Special Markets Department, Random House, Inc., 1540 Broadway, New York, NY 10036.

BROADWAY BOOKS and its logo, a letter B bisected on the diagonal, are trademarks of Broadway Books, a division of Random House, Inc.

First Broadway Books trade paperback edition published 2001.

Designed by Claire Naylon Vaccaro
Illustrated by Marianne Rankin

Library of Congress Cataloging-in-Publication Data
French, Hal W.
Zen and the art of anything/Hal W. French; illustrations by Marianne Rankin.
p. cm.
Originally published: Columbia, S.C. : Summerhouse Press, 1999.
Includes bibliographical references.
1. Religious life—Zen Buddhism. 2. Zen Buddhism—Influence. 3. Arts, Zen. I. Title.
BQ9286 .F75 2001
294.3'927—dc21

2001018131

ISBN 0-7679-07973
01 02 03 04 05 10 9 8 7 6 5 4 3 2 1

Contents

A Zen Foreword for a Zen Book by Kuang-ming Wu   *xiii*

CHAPTER I: MY STORY AND THIS BOOK   *1*

CHAPTER II: BREATHING AND SPEAKING   *19*

CHAPTER III: WAKING AND SLEEPING   *36*

CHAPTER IV: MOVING AND STAYING   *50*

CHAPTER V: EATING AND DRINKING   *65*

CHAPTER VI: PLAYING AND WORKING   *82*

CHAPTER VII: CARING AND LOVING   *99*

CHAPTER VIII: THRIVING AND SURVIVING   *117*

Epilogue   *133*

Acknowledgments   *134*

For Further Reading   *137*

DEDICATION

To Gene Doyle,
who knew so much of Zen before he studied it formally,
and who taught us so much beyond his tragic death in 1996.

A NOTE TO THE READER

The reader may appreciate a word about this book's format.
I've often felt that reading can be a chore,
since our eyes and minds don't readily adapt to the rigidities
of justified margins, which break up phrases and ideas,
forcing us to drop our eyes arbitrarily, awkwardly, to the next line.
The attempt here is to make those line jumps more natural, in structure
and reason.

I hope this style may make your reading more pleasant,
and render Zen more accessible.

A Zen Foreword
for a Zen Book

Is my baby a boy, a girl, or neuter? No, none of these. Is it celibate, then? Not quite, for it giggles curiously at sex. Baby is sex's climax, sex-interested, and belongs to no particular sex. It simply is. My baby is my parent. Coming home to my baby, I come home to Me.

Such homecoming is "nothing special," Professor French assures us. When I give up my sophisticated adult thinking, I quit stupefying myself and others, and I come home to life's Prime, its Beginning. It feels so good, spellbound in frisky babies' "show and tell," learning their laughing lifeless art. They "can do anything," as they say, for they never fight the river; they just frolic in it, flow with it. I now join in my baby's nimble "art of anything," to quote Professor French's phrase.

Being artless is not an art, nor does it deny art. It simply charms anything anywhere. Professor French artlessly presents this mighty "non-art of anything," the Beginner's Mind, my Baby's feisty Heart and deft Hand. This book simply flows, flows simply, and gently cleanses me of daily eddies of hustle and bustle. The book delights as my baby, just being there. Professor French calls such non-art "zen," perhaps a non-Zen, not awesome Zen.

I was released into Me as I read through the book at a sitting, for I could not put it down. This is a book of my Baby, Me, who "can do anything." You will not be able to get over this book, either. How could anyone get over oneself, one's Me, irresistible as one's own baby? The book shows my Baby, sparkling with surprising insights—feisty as my adorable baby, fresh as my baby's adoring eyes. This book is simply irresistible.

Kuang-ming Wu
Author of *The Butterfly as Companion*

My Story and This Book

MY STORY

The year was 1990, and I was presenting a paper on Zen at a Buddhism conference
in southern Taiwan. In the course of the paper,
I made a passing reference to Bodhidharma,
the traditional bringer of Zen to China from India.

After the presentation, a resident Buddhist monk approached me, and,
with a whimsical smile, pointed to me, and said,
"You are Bodhidharma!"
I was rather pleasantly mystified by that, but could elicit no further elaboration.
The monk simply left, and I was left to ponder the classic Zen *koan*, or riddle:
"Why has Bodhidharma come from the West?"
And why, then, had I come from the West to talk to a largely Buddhist audience,
about Zen?
In what way was I, late in time, following Bodhidharma's model?
And why, as a Westerner, several years later, should I attempt a book
about Zen?
I am in many ways an unlikely candidate for such a project.
First, I'm an academic, and academics don't write much about Zen.
They may study about it, and teach a small segment or even a rare course about it,
but they don't write about it.
Practitioners do.
Professors write about lots of things religious,
but not much on Zen.
The ones who write about Zen are persons, East and West,
who have spent years in Zen centers and monasteries,
who have received extensive training with Zen masters,
and have been initiated.
I understand that, and am intimidated.

Second, it isn't just the profession, it's personal.
I'm a still more unlikely candidate by way of origins.
So I'm still more intimidated.
But this isn't an expert's book on esoteric Zen.
That might intimidate you, too.

Zen here is "nothing special,"
for "nothing special" people like you and me.

I have to pick up the story a little more than a century ago,
to detail my own journey toward wanting to write about Zen.

On September 1893, over 100,000 people lined up
to cross the border into a section of Oklahoma known as the Cherokee Strip.
Other segments of the Indian Territory were opened a few years earlier and later,
but this was the largest and the most dramatic such entry.
My grandfather was among those who raced to establish a claim.
It was in many ways the closing of a frontier.
Five days earlier, in Chicago, the World's Parliament of Religions had opened.
It was, in many ways, the opening of an incredible new frontier.

My early life was shaped much more by the first event.

Perhaps my grandfather's horse was slow.
At any rate, the land he claimed was poor,
and he came back in a few years to settle in Kansas with his family,
having buried two small boys in the soil of Oklahoma.
As the Indian Territories were opened for settling,
the frontier closed.
Yet, by the time I appeared, elements of it remained.

We lived, in my boyhood, in a small town near Dodge City, "Land of the Fast Draw."
The lore of the cowboy was a living thing,
not just memorialized in the graves at nearby Boot Hill.

The most visible markers in Mullinville, my town,
were windmills and grain elevators.
My father operated one of the elevators, and my mother had taught home economics,
which gave me an early appreciation for wonderful basic cooking,
a subject for further discussion in chapter five.
The vital church in Mullinville, just across the street from our home,
had a strong measure of frontier Christianity,
evangelical in style and content.
It was, and its impress remains, whatever else has been appended,
very important to me.

I did my first public speaking as an early teenager
in a contest sponsored by the WCTU, the Women's Christian Temperance Union.
It was a respectable, sedate group.
Its founder, crusading, saloon-smashing Carry A. Nation,
less than forty years before, had been based in Medicine Lodge,
only a little farther away than Dodge City, in the other direction.
That was my boyhood, growing up in a farming community
in dustbowl, depression days,
with some residual legacies of the frontier still around.

While some of those frontiers remained open for me,
some other far different ones were beckoning in young adulthood,
grafting themselves onto my own root stock.
But it was not until 1966, sixty-three years after the Parliament of Religions,
that I really awakened,
while studying one summer at the University of Chicago,
to the awareness of that event and all that it meant.
Research on the Parliament and one of its leading figures, Swami Vivekananda,

opened to me the world of Eastern wisdom, and that door has kept opening wider.
It led me to Zen.

The religion of South Asia became my primary research area,
but East Asian religion was on my teaching platter, too,
and travel to East Asia deepened the interest.
Most notably, a personal friend and mentor,
Professor Nolan P. Jacobson, quickened that interest.
His books, his lively presentations made me want to know more about Japan and Zen.
With his death in 1987,
and the subsequent invitation to write a chapter in a memorial volume to him,
I knew what I'd contribute.
My chapter, the essay "Zen and the Art of Anything,"
written that same year, was the initiation of a serious study of Zen for me.
Other papers followed, and more travel in East Asia,
with visits to Zen centers,
and by 1994 I felt ready to offer a course for Honors and M.A. students,
again with the same title.
Several days in the Green Gulch Zen Farm were very helpful,
and the book *Zen Mind, Beginner's Mind,* by Shunryu Suzuki,
founder of the San Francisco Zen Center that spawned nearby Green Gulch,
was my favorite Zen source.
My students, each time I've taught the course in the University and elsewhere,
have actualized his title: they've been incredible co-teachers and learners—
more than in any course I've ever taught.
We were all beginners, and that democratic Zen spirit
fostered more of a workshop than a classroom environment,
with everybody contributing.

Suzuki refers in his book to the example of his master,
who had joined the Soto Zen order when he was thirty, which is rather late.
And Suzuki shares how his master's teacher would often,
both scoldingly and endearingly, refer to him as "You lately-joined fellow."
What then of me?
To modify the cliché, "When he was my age,
he had been alive for thirty years!"
I have come much later to the feast,
and that might be another inhibiting feature.
But Suzuki gave me the challenge of recognizing and speaking
precisely from my beginner's mind-set.
Is there any validity to a beginner's observations?
Can an outsider's freshness of perspective contribute to the discourse,
along with the seasoned wisdom of the insider, long immersed in the tradition?
And if the outsider has been more of an insider in other practices,
can he also bring a useful comparative vantage point to the table?

Suzuki's emphasis on practice and process spoke to me, also;
other sources seemed too goal-oriented, too focused on getting there,
to the all-embracing state called *kensho*, or *satori*:

ENLIGHTENMENT!

Some told stories of enlightenment experiences in Japanese Zen monasteries,
but made it clear that no content could be communicated,
for that would take away from the search of other aspirants.
That part left me cold.
I remembered from childhood the teasing jingle,

"I know something I won't tell,"
and I remember resenting it when my father, a member of the Masonic Lodge,
reluctantly said that he couldn't tell me, his son,
about what went on in the Masonic sessions.
I think that I developed an early distrust of the esoteric,
the too tightly held conclusions of any spiritual or fraternal elite.
What appealed to me about Zen, instead,
and in sharp contrast, was precisely

ITS ACCESSIBILITY.

Yes, the reading of Zen sources, time spent in Zendos,
disciplined meditative practice were important for me.
But factors like these are necessary in gaining insight into any religious tradition.
You can't become an insider through study alone,
you need to get an understanding of the experience of an insider,
and to appropriate what elements you can.
What amazed me, despite the esoteric trappings that had so often intimidated me,
was my experience that I could learn something of Zen.
That was itself an "enlightening" realization!
An "outsider" could get into Zen, even one who came from rustic origins
only slightly removed from the frontier of the American West!
Amazing!
And if I could, then that says something about Zen, not just about me.
Zen is far more accessible than some would lead us to believe.
And I don't have to claim, in writing about it,
that I live now in the state of total enlightenment.

There is a delightful story told by Huston Smith in his preface to Suzuki's book
Zen Mind, Beginner's Mind.
Smith notes, "In Shunryu Suzuki's book the words *satori* and *kensho*,
its near equivalent, never appear." And then Smith shares a story:
"When, four months before his death, I had the opportunity to ask him
why *satori* didn't figure in his book, his wife leaned toward me and
whispered impishly, 'It's because he hasn't had it'; whereupon the
roshi batted his fan at her in mock consternation and with finger to
his lips hissed, 'Shhhh! Don't tell him!' When our laughter had
subsided, he said simply, 'It's not that *satori* is unimportant, but
it's not the part of Zen that needs to be stressed.' "

That is so charmingly wise. I would prefer to talk about enlightening moments,
rather than a state of enlightenment, and when such moments come,
to feel that these should be shared.
The man whom we call The Buddha would, I think, have disclaimed the title.
It's *"nothing special."*
It means simply "One who woke up,"
and he made it clear that the rest of us could wake up, too.
Chapter three of this book includes what seemed literally like a wake-up insight
for me, coming as it did in the middle of the night.
I had for days been pondering the themes of *kronos* and *kairos,*
clock time and timing, while writing that chapter,
when suddenly I woke at two A.M. on a day in October, 1997,
the moment that the time changed from Eastern Daylight to Eastern Standard Time.
It seemed, in that luminous moment,
that I now understood something that had always seemed impossibly obscure.
I felt, just then, that I knew about the relativity of time,

and that I had known it all along,
Later I learned that my wife, at that same hour, Greenwich Mean Time,
had left her hotel in London to fly back home.
Three zones, intersecting:

"What time is it?"
"It depends."

And I am aware that every time you use that phrase, you know about relativity, too.
No esoteric secrets here. *"Nothing special."*
And if that feels like at least SMALL-CASE enlightenment,
so be it.
Perhaps any student of Zen, like Bodhidharma himself, has an obligation
to share something of what he has experienced.
And if a few SMALL-CASE enlightenment moments should occur for you,
in transit with me, in these pages, then you can share those, too.

"You are Bodhidharma."

THIS BOOK

Why, indeed, should I write, or you read, yet another book on this theme?
The premise has spawned an extensive genre:
Zen and (or *Zen in*) *the Art of . . .*
Let me count the ways:
Perhaps the two most familiar are Eugen Herrigel's classic *Zen in the Art of Archery*,
and Robert Pirsig's cult favorite from the early seventies,

Zen and the Art of Motorcycle Maintenance.
But simply to enumerate a few others, the list may include:
Zen and the Art of Calligraphy, Zen and the Art of Writing,
A Beginner's Guide to Zen and the Art of Windsurfing,
Zen and the Art of the Macintosh, Zen and the Art of the Internet,
Zen and the Art of Medicaid, Zen in the Martial Arts,
Zen in the Art of Flower Arrangement, Zen in the Art of J. D. Salinger.
If we were to add other titles, just *Zen and . . .*, dropping the *Art,*
or still others, associating Zen with other pursuits,
the list would grow exponentially.
Why have these books multiplied? What is the premise behind them?
One answer may simply be trivialization, using a catchy title to sell a non-book,
by appending the word *Zen* and appropriating its popular mystique
for marketing purposes.
The resultant product may have little to do with Zen,
and contain little of substance about the subject itself.
Or it may seem exploitative,
separating a specialized activity from the original tradition,
which sought to cultivate a holistic approach to life.
In a similar way, other Eastern disciplines have been popularized,
tailored to partial interests,
as in *Yoga for Skiers,* or *How Now, Tao Jones?*
But even these pop market titles may indicate two truths about the traditions themselves:
First, they are portable.
There is an element of universality about them.
They are not culture-bound to the world of the East.
And second, they can, with authenticity, be applied to various life pursuits.

Zen simply means meditation.

The first premise of this book, then,
which it may hold in common with some of the titles listed above,
is that a wide variety of life pursuits,
when combined with a meditative and mindful discipline,
may be elevated to the level of art forms.
And, while this premise claims the portability and universality
that properly belong to Zen,
the applicability factor is authentically present within Japan itself,
the originating culture that we most readily associate with Zen.
I refer to the classical *"do"* patterns of Japan, indicated by the suffix ending,
as these describe particularly intense life disciplines.
Do, derived from *Tao*, or way, is abundantly evidenced,
as in the way of tea *(chado)*, the way of soft combat *(judo)*,
the way of calligraphy *(shodo)*, the way of the samurai *(bushido)*,
the way of flower arranging *(ikebana* or *kado)*, the way of fencing *(kendo)*,
the way of archery *(kyudo)*.
Many other skills might be added to this list,
such as landscape gardening, dramatic arts, ceramics, weaving, and the like.

I once witnessed in a home near Hiroshima
many specimens of the art of rock carving and polishing,
which added beautifully to the decor.
In all of these we see, more than the production of specific attractive objects,
a deep expression of innate creativity.
The objects appear to grow with integrity
out of the highest refinement of the artisan's human spirit.

The artisans may become designated as "National Treasures,"
not merely to be accorded near veneration,
but to inspire and instruct others who have novice status on a particular path.

This may illustrate, in brief, the artistic legacy that characterizes Japan,
but how do we establish the specific contribution of Zen to this climate?
That isn't easy, since several traditions factor in,
most notably Shinto, Taoism, Zen and other schools of Buddhism,
along with the disciplines of Confucianism.
Several of these traditions derive from originals borrowed from China,
sometimes through a Korean filter,
and Buddhist forms are traceable, in some cases, further back still, to India.
Richard Walker, a colleague, long-time student of East Asia,
and former ambassador to Korea,
once suggested a conundrum to me that may be useful here
in understanding both Japan and Zen.
It's simply the word *ad_pt.*
Fill the blank for the first term characterizing Japan with the letter *o,*
rendering the word *adopt.*

The Japanese have been called the world's greatest borrowers.
It is a notion which accords well with the Buddhist teaching of emptiness,
which can simply be defined as openness,
a willingness in this case to absorb from strange systems,
to drink from alien wells.
The Japanese word *torukumu,* "to take over," similarly expresses this ideal:
a capacity for spiritual ingestion.
Emptiness implies an invitation to be filled,

a welcome to what is offered by a myriad of potential hosts.

Shinto itself, the religion native to Japan,

was given much of its shape, and its actual name, through Chinese influence,

with the term *Shinto* derived from *shen-tao*,

the Chinese word for the way of nature (yet another *do* pattern).

But the borrowed elements blend with other elements,

indigenizing themselves into what is termed *Nihon-do*, or, simply, the way of Japan.

Nihon-do means no slavish imitation,

but that any borrowed elements soon lose their strangeness

in the peculiarly Japanese mix.

The second variation on the conundrum, then, inserts the letter *a*,

forming the world *adapt*.

Religiously, the different traditions cited, along with folk and popular religion,

all contribute to the Japanese mix.

Clearly it isn't simple, then, to isolate the unique contribution of Zen,

except to say that it seems to have provided, historically,

a strong stimulus to aesthetic sensibility and artistic expression.

We think of the poetic form of *haiku*,

a favorite, concise way of conveying, in a singular, sharp image,

a profound impression from some experience of nature,

or of the *koan*, a riddle which impels the adept to look deeper,

behind the surface nonsense of a given paradox.

The Trappist writer Thomas Merton once observed,

"We find very serious and responsible practitioners of Zen

first denying that it is religion, then denying that it is a sect or school,

and finally denying that it is confined to Buddhism and its structure."

While this conclusion may again make it difficult to establish Zen "influence,"
it may indicate that Zen's own absence of institutional walls
is congruent with the Japanese spirit,
allowing it to blend borrowed elements, indigenizing,
stamping them with a characteristic Japanese spirit.

The third letter to be added to the conundrum has doubtless been anticipated,
with the new word, formed by adding the letter *e*, being *adept*.
That which is borrowed and indigenized then enables persons,
in the Japanese setting, to become more *adept* at the practice
than those from whom it was originally borrowed.

Without analyzing this notion, a simple anecdote,
with which everyone is familiar, may serve to illustrate.
How is it that such a profound change, in half a century, has occurred,
by which the label "Made in Japan,"
formerly attached to a small, cheap trinket,
now identifies a sophisticated technological product?
One thinks immediately of various brand names,
and associations which they convey:
Sony, Mazda, Nikon, Fuji, Nissan, Honda, Toyota, and others.
These convey images of intricate electronic equipment,
state-of-the-art cameras and computers, superior automobiles.

Japan's modern miracle is dramatized as we compare it, for instance,
with Brazil, a country of roughly the same population, around 125 million persons.
On paper, Japan has all the disadvantages:
an island with few natural resources

compared to Brazil's thousands of square miles of arable land
and abundant mineral deposits.
And yet a recent statistic shows Japan accounting for ten percent
of the gross world product, while Brazil accounts for less than one percent.
How has this miracle been achieved? Let it stand, as is.
Every reader will recognize the amazing recovery of Japan since World War II.
The "adept" quality is profoundly evident.

An additional feature to note:
all of the Japanese art forms that have been cited,
as well as others for which we may need to generate new terms,
such as *techni-do*,
must be seen as growing out of a general quality of life.
To illustrate from one of the classical *do* patterns,
we may note that the place where *kendo* was practiced in ancient times
was called "the place of enlightenment."
That place for most is not necessarily where a "fine" art is cultivated,
but the work place *(techni-do* again), the play place,
the home place, where we may simply pursue the way of being human.
What we are after, then, is the pursuit of what might be called "lower education,"
not higher, the quest for the mastery of the common arts, not the fine ones.

Here it must be recognized that "arts" themselves may be abused,
and that Zen, like any other tool, or "means of grace,"
can be exploited, as Brian Victoria has detailed in his recent book, *Zen at War.*
The Japanese war machine, in World War II,
used some Zen disciplines to cultivate incredibly dehumanizing mind-sets,
which resulted in horribly brutal atrocities in places like Nanjing, China.

The approach of this book, then,
is to suggest that the arts pursued must not be employed
for ego-enhancement or for selfish purposes,
nor may they be separated from the mundane tasks
that integrate us with the human community.
An *enabling* book must also *ennoble*.

The second major premise of this book, then
(and what may distinguish it from the titles mentioned above),
is that a meditative and mindful approach to these common arts
that we customarily take for granted
may enable us to live total, not just segmental
lives which are more generally and authentically human.

"Fine" arts, or specialized expressions of excellence, may emerge from this base,
but we may experience an expanded and enhanced appreciation
for what it means simply to be alive.
You are invited to understand Zen as something that is not exotic,
but the most mundane, practical approach to life that is conceivable.
It is a vehicle to everyday spirituality.
As R. H. Blyth reminds us, "When sacred really equals profane, we have Zen."
That means that we will focus here on the tasks that each of us performs,
daily (or regularly, or routinely),
but so very seldom does in a mindful, reflective way:
breathing and speaking, waking and sleeping,
moving and staying, eating and drinking,
playing and working, caring and loving,
thriving and surviving.

These are birth-to-death, life-cycle activities in which we all engage.
Can they be elevated to art forms?

The book's third premise, then, an elaboration of the second,
is built on the reversibility of the conundrum cited above,
namely that the mindful, meditative disciplines of Zen
may be *adopted* by persons of any culture,
adapted non-intrusively into their life-styles,
with the result that these persons, in all or any of their life pursuits
may become more *adept* in their practice of them,
to the benefit of all.

That's the claim.

I once had a student, David Sims, who was taking an independent study in Sanskrit
with me while he was also enrolled in structured courses
in Greek, Hebrew, Latin, Arabic, and Chinese.
Impressive!
I thought, of course, that he must be aspiring
to become a consummate classical linguist,
but his vocational ambition was to become a house painter.
He simply wanted to have some facility for the rest of his life,
whatever he did vocationally,
to study the great religious traditions in their original languages.
His was the purest liberal arts ideal I've ever encountered.
In fact, he didn't become a house painter, but a plumber, and a good one.
A personal reference: he's often worked for me!
Maybe he picked up naturally, with reference to classical languages,

the concluding insight of Marian Mountain's book *The Zen Environment,*
when she observed, simply,
"Zen is a plumber's helper."
The most mundane tool for the most practical of tasks:

See if it helps you.

II

BREATHING AND
SPEAKING

BREATHING

Where do we begin?

Why not where life begins, with breathing?

So breathe. Just breathe.
For the next two minutes, or about twenty-five breaths, perhaps,
just breathe, before you read further, and be aware of each breath.

You've borrowed or bought this book,
and you've just begun to match that investment with your own attention

to the most basic of all activities,

the act of breathing.

That's where Zen and about every school of meditation that I know of begins.

Where else?

Think of a baby's first breath, and your own next breath.

You enter life, life enters your body, with each inhalation.

It's like each beat of your heart in being largely involuntary.

But unlike your heartbeat, your breathing can easily enter your awareness.

It's that initial consciousness of your breathing that becomes the first building block

to a heightened awareness of many other facets of your life.

Your alertness expands,

and you begin to marvel at the mundane moments that fill each day.

So, just breathe.

You seldom need to gasp for breath;

there's a ready quantity of air around you, which sustains you.

You are concerned at times about the quality of that air,

but you're not on the Mir spacecraft,

where your oxygen supply is threatened by a system shutdown,

or living in Tokyo, where, as relief from air pollution,

you might pop into an oxygen bar.

Usually, for most of us, the air is there, as a cherished given.

Recent findings in North America suggest that it's actually improving.

But if the air supply immediately around you is polluted, say, from cigarette smoke,

see if you can remove the smoke or move away from it as you continue this exercise.

Some would seek to enhance meditative moments with incense,

giving a sacred, set-apart feeling.

Or you may simply prefer natural air,
ideally, weather permitting, air outside or entering your room from outside.
You need breathing room,
and maybe a habitual breathing room in your house, for meditation.
As the Vietnamese Buddhist monk Thich Nhat Hanh suggests,
a bell which a person entering that room for meditation employs
may signal others, and invite them, where they are,
to breathe also, and the moments of peace may spread through the house.
The space itself, consciously chosen, can be sanctified.
"Where we breathe, we bow," in the poet Gary Snyder's words.

In Zen, the breathing is part of the practice of *zazen*, or seated meditation.
You may want to enhance your intentionality by acquiring a *zafu*,
or firm, round cushion, for this purpose,
and consulting a manual of instruction on matters of posture if these aren't familiar.
But details of practice may be suggestive and not dogmatic,
so you may evolve into your own style,
with variations on procedures followed in a given school.
We will thus be discussing *zen* (lowercase),
simply meaning meditation, as much as
Zen, which might refer to a particular Japanese model.
It will be helpful to know the Zen tradition, and to spend time in a Zen community,
but the approach here is that, as claimed above,
you may *adapt* the tradition to your own circumstances.
This does not mean sanctioning a casual, careless approach,
but a discipline that is your own.
Back to breathing.
As you breathe, you breathe with Beethoven and Buddha, with Mary and with Socrates.

It's the same substance, the same air.

You are sustained by this regular pattern of the filling and emptying,

the rising and falling of your lungs.

If you began, as suggested, with two minutes of attention to your breathing, consider:

assuming that your rate of breathing is about like mine,

twenty-five breaths for two minutes,

that adds up to the incredible total of 18,000 breaths each day!

Are you amazed?

18,000 inhalations, 18,000 exhalations,

the exchange of oxygen for carbon dioxide

(simply stated; of course it's more complex),

repeated these many, many times every day!

Each of us moves, by some estimations, about 440 cubic feet of air per day.

We are working, just by breathing!

In my customary twenty minutes of morning meditation,

I am focusing on just over one percent of my 18,000 daily breaths.

I modify the sacred phrase only slightly, to ask: "Give us this day our daily breaths,"

and seek to expand my awareness and appreciation of those breaths.

And in my state of South Carolina,

the reflection is canonized and expanded in the state motto:

"Dum spiro spero": "While I breathe, I hope."

I am, literally, "inspired," by each inbreath.

And with it I hope for . . . what?

Minimally, another breath, and another, and so much more.

But before you elaborate on your own hopes,

just center on your present breathing process.

What is implied in the common phrase "Don't hold your breath"?

Maybe it means, "Don't put your life on hold
till something that you want to happen occurs.
That something may be extremely unlikely,
but in any case, that's a future event,
and now is where you are.
Don't hold your breath waiting for something else."

Fix your mind on the image of a digital watch or clock.
That's the image of your mind in meditation.
The digital instrument has no sense of past or future;
all it has is the moment.
You've doubtless watched it to see how it changes.
Take it as a challenge, in the memorable words of a beloved friend,
the late Dr. Nolan Jacobson,
"to catch the ceaseless flow of quality in the passing moment."
You have no agenda; simply count your breaths,
watch your breathing.
How much quality can you compress into that moment,
and each passing moment of your life by simply being there and nowhere else,
giving yourself completely to the possibilities resident within it?
Try the simple exercise suggested by Thich Nhat Hanh:
"Breathing in, I calm my body.
Breathing out, I smile."
Stay with that for several breaths. Let it penetrate.

"*Dum spiro, spero,*" again. "While I breathe, I hope."
But reduce that hope, which seems like a futurist category,
to the most immediately present tense possible,

simply the hope for your watched-for next breath,

that while your attention is focused on the breathing process,

it will last long enough for you to learn from it:

just the next breath.

You hope that your life will be supported,

that your breathing apparatus will not fail,

that the supply of oxygen will not suddenly dry up or be poisoned.

You will expire someday, but not yet,

as you now expire in your next outbreath or "little death" expiration.

Revel in the momentary experience of breathing.

You're alive!!

Once more, as you're reflecting, this miracle may again impress itself upon you.

In the sense of wonder that they create,

our moments of meditation, of focusing on our breathing,

may seem more and more like prayer.

But as you breathe, move out a little from the immediacy of your time zone,

to identify with others who are breathing with you,

and all who will pick up the cadence of breathing after your own ceases.

The ancients; all who have ever lived,

and have breathed their last.

All who will populate this earth space in the unimaginable days to come.

And feel how the tapestry of breaths is now being shaped

by the contrasting rhythms of all the life forms that are breathing with you.

Feel the contrasting rates of breathing themselves,

determined partly by genus and species, partly by activity.

Your own breathing is now, doubtless, relaxed, regular and tranquil.

But hear, also,

the labored breathing of the sick and dying,

the escalated breathing of workers in strenuous labor,
or of the athlete in competition,
the quickened breaths of passion,
the almost silenced breathing of those in great fear,
perhaps in hiding, paralyzed by worry that their next breath,
however slight, might betray their presence.

Hear . . .
the hushed breath of wonder,
the excitement that takes your breath away.
Remember, and remember how you recovered
from having the wind knocked out of you,
feeling the surge of air once again enter your lungs.
And remember,
how in near panic, close to drowning,
you fought for your life,
breaking the surface of the water,
knowing, in vast relief,
what a gift it is to breathe.
Remember now,
in the quiet of this moment.
And cherish the gift.
And consider yourself as proxy, in your cherishing,
for all those life-forms which cannot reflect and marvel,
as you can, at the givenness of the stable supply of air which sustains them.

As you are grateful for the diversity of life,
in its myriad manifestations,
you are now the celebrant for all of these.

It is a priestly act,
and your role is that of priest for all receivers of the air that surrounds you.
As a human, do you believe in your priesthood for all these receivers?
You may, then, want to lift your hands now, symbolically,
and swell your lungs, as you lift these creatures up with your breathing,
celebrating all of the realized possibilities,
the fantastic varieties of living things,
over measureless time, beyond your imaginings.
Consider, in Gary Snyder's memorable phrase, all
"Us critters hanging out together something like two billion years.
At the end of the ice age
we are the bears, we are the ravens."

Breathing is always a sharing, a communication:
"in and out," or "out-in" (*kokyu* in Japanese).
Breathing out we give life to trees;
Breathing in we receive life from them.

Link this moment, then, with the further reaches of time and space;
right now, as you breathe,
"The ringing in your ears
Is the cricket in the stars."
How do we fathom the magnitude of these identities forged now,
in our breathing, with all these creatures?
What are the mechanisms, the dynamisms, by which they ingest air?
Perhaps the question intrudes now,
but it may on another occasion impel my search for greater knowledge,
and also for a deepening reverence for the Mysteries
that will always elude my most dedicated quest.

And these Mysteries include the wind,

that exterior force which matches my own breath dynamism.

What forces energize and pattern the movement of the winds?

Consider, as you have mused over breath patterns, the winds, also:

The howling gale, driving rain before it,

leveling objects in its path,

churning tumultuous ocean waves,

the quiet spring morning,

in which scarcely a leaf rustles in the gentlest of breezes,

the north winds of late autumn,

with their warning of icy blasts to come,

the soft sighing of the trees on a summer evening,

cooling the heat rising from city streets,

And all of these, metaphors for the divine activity in our midst,

the spirit itself:

"The wind blows where it will, and you hear the sound of it,

but you do not know whence it comes or whither it goes."

Mystery again.

But we are given a clue as to origins.

The same Greek word is employed both for wind and spirit.

Play still other word games with me for a moment.

Go back to the Hebrew Bible,

to the account of the creation of human life:

"And God breathed into his nostrils the breath of life, and man became a living soul."

Three Hebrew words for breath are used in this partial verse,

each reinforcing the other with the clear conclusion:

Life is breath; breath is life.

So in Japan, the *hara*, the mid-section, or center of breathing, is the locus of life.
That locus may be thought of, alternatively, as the nerve center, the brain,
where mental activity is "*head*quartered,"
or the blood circulatory center, the heart,
which is our mythic romantic core.
Japan combines them in *kokoro*, or "heartmind."
And it's fitting that Zen, which focuses on breathing,
would blossom in Japan, where the *hara*
(as in *hara-kiri*, the act by which, in classical samurai spirit,
the warrior may choose to end his life at its center, the *hara*)
also embodies the essence of human life.

And back to the Hebrew,
where the most sacred name for the Divine contains only consonants,
the word rendered in the most recent English translations of scripture as *Yahweh*.
In the Hebrew, vowels were not used, and the word was too sacred to be pronounced.
Assumed vowels were inserted between other consonants, and articulated as *Adonai*.
But consider the consonants in the sacred word itself,
called the Tetragrammaton:
they are perhaps the softest of consonants,
which may be transliterated as *yodh, heh, waw, heh*.
Each one can almost be breathed.
Is the insight here, then, that the Divine may best be represented in breath or wind?
It would seem so.
And my relation to the Divine, also, carries this same flavor:
consider—while we're looking at words—
that in three classical languages, Sanskrit, Hebrew, Greek,
four words, translated into English as "breath" and "wind," "soul" and "spirit,"

are so closely related,
the intimate to the Ultimate, the breath of my soul to the winds of the Spirit.
And Kuang-ming Wu reminds us that the Chinese, also, in Chuang Tzu,
also link these forces, in the "three pipings" of man, earth, and heaven.

In each tradition, then, this affirmation, with each breath:
I ingest the cosmos: *I ingest the cosmos!*
I borrow, for an instant, the tiniest fragment of it, and perhaps,
in the most miniscule way imaginable, my life,
symbolized by my outbreath, enriches its workings.
Maybe. And maybe by more than mere chemical exchange.
Is that arrogance, or simply the consciousness of belonging, participating?

As you return, then, to an awareness of your breathing,
think of the cumulative consciousness that your attention has already given you:
in each breath, you identify, across time and space,
with your neighbor, who breathes, and your distant ancestor,
whose lungs were filled with the selfsame air that fills yours now,
And with the squirrel that scampers across your patio,
and pauses for a moment, to breathe with you,
And with the robin that comes to your bird feeder,
halts his messy eating for a fraction of a second,
and breathes invisibly, by a different mechanism from your own,
And with the wind, which blows mysteriously
in its various directions, with varied intensities,
And with the Divine itself,
whose physical form, since we must imagine some such manifestation,
is best symbolized forcefully by wind, and subtly by breath.

(The first creation account in Genesis:
"And the Spirit of God moved upon the face of the waters.")
As you breathe, you are spirit, you are inspired.
Consider the alternate words for breath, then.
Inhalation, yes, but also *inspiration.*
Exhalation, yes, but also *expiration.*
Every in-breath a little life; every out-breath a little death.
But the process doesn't have a morbid connotation:
you receive life, you give life.
In what ways do you receive life? In what ways do you give it?
Are these subjects for meditation?

Breath...
It's celebrated in romantic lyrics—
"With every breath I take,"
"And every breath an inspiration,"
"You are the breathless hush of evening..."
And if it isn't quite breathless,
it's still that most subtle moment which in its quiet reverence becomes magical.
Go further with breath in your own word associations...
and then take it a step still further—
breath, as a precondition for...

SPEAKING

You can sing your breath, as in the lines above;
love lyrics, oratorios of praise, unison chants, singing the blues.
Or you can speak it, in words.
That's what song or speech is: consciously shaped breath, on the outbreath
(always on the outbreath. Try it on the inbreath.
You can do it, but in very short phrases, and it sounds strangled).
Breath, which becomes language, intentionally formed,
for expressive, communicative purposes.
I am not now thinking of the incessant chatter of the compulsively garrulous,
or of the insensitive, careless and crude vulgarity
which profanes the idea of speech itself.
But the word, which mirrors the creative power of the Word itself.

The Word goes forth: "Let there be . . ." and worlds are brought into being.
The Word goes forth—"Peace, be still—"
and winds and waves,
and fear-filled hearts of fishermen on a storm-tossed inland sea are quieted.
Consider known masters of language
who have moved masses through oratorical power:
Demosthenes,
maybe mythically refining his tongue's skills by speaking through a mouthful of pebbles;
Daniel Webster,
who in a whimsical revision of the Faustian legend
could defeat the devil
by mustering and delivering the best possible defense for the soul of a man;
or all the Shakespearean soliloquies,
inviting us through their eloquence
to ponder the grandeur and misery of the human condition;
Lincoln, at Gettysburg,
whose words hallowed the sacrifices made for the vision of a united nation;
Martin Luther King,
and the dream that he shared, and challenged us all to actualize;
Maya Angelou,
who has taught us in the richness of her language
and the force of her presence,
how to hear the Song of the Caged Bird.

Consider these,
and hear also the incredible energy of the collective voices of fans in a football stadium,
celebrating a game-winning touchdown,
Or the electrifying presence of a rock star,

whose amplified voice and high-tech hype

generates such amazing decibels of resonant sound from the youthful audience!

That's the gift of speech,

in some of its most dramatic expressions,

in historic time, and in our time.

But you, also, have the gift of speech.

You, also, can create, can comfort and empower

through your own consciously shaped breath: speech.

Remembering the masters and movers in the realm of speech and language

is not intended to intimidate, but to inspire.

What are the possibilities of speech?

A beloved teacher, Edwin Prince Booth, once recalled to our classroom

a scene from childhood. He was on an outing with his father.

They had just finished their picnic lunch, and he had wandered off,

while his father was clearing up the lunch site.

Suddenly, the attention of both father and son was alerted

by a whistle blast from an approaching train.

The father saw where the son was playing, atop the nearby trestle,

paralyzed in that instant by fear,

his eyes riveted to the onrushing locomotive.

The distance was too great to cover,

but the father's voice crossed it in a moment:

"Edwin, jump!!"

And the son, energized by his father's voice, jumped to safety.

Those two words,

doubtless the most important ones spoken in the father's lifetime,

gave life to his son.

You can give life in your speech.
You can diminish life when you speak in hatred or anger.
Consciously shaped breath, again, on the outbreath.
Inspiration, the inbreath; expiration, the outbreath.
You give up something of your life, you expire, in your speech.
The life/death alternation, again.
But you are shaping that little death into something that can give life to another.
When you are not on speaking terms with someone else,
you are withholding your life from that person.
"Don't hold your breath: don't withhold your speech."
Yet another lesson.

Do my words come from the depths of truth?
Vac, or True Speech, is one of the Vedic gods in Hinduism,
just as the *Logos*, the Word,
is venerated as the expressive nature of the Divine in the West.
Is my own speech true? Is it life-giving?
The other side of the coin, of course, is hearing.
I have no right to speak to one to whom I am not willing to listen.
The gift is dialogic.
Often I am called simply to conduct a listening witness,
by my quiet, receptive presence.
Listening is speech on the inbreath, breathing others in,
developing a capacity for *inloquence*, effective listening,
as much as *eloquence*, the art of speaking.

It is hard for me, similarly, to imagine meditation so pure, so focused,
that is not attuned to what the air that I breathe also brings to me:

the sounds of nature.
The hymn celebrates it:
"All nature sings, And round me rings
The music of the spheres."
A sensitive nine-year-old expresses it:
"The sound roaming over me
breathes steadily."
"He that hath ears to hear, let him hear."

You are, then, in your speech,
welcoming the intelligent, intelligible voice of your neighbor in response,
and engaging in discourse, back and forth.
You are, in your breathing,
feeling the swelling of the earth's lungs,
the air coursing through living tissues,
and given voice now, to your hearing.
These enter your meditation, and help to shape it.
You are aware, and you are grateful.

Zen: meditation.
It is no alien word, but one which we are destined to refine, to discipline,
with its companion word, *mindfulness,*
until they become our most natural art forms.
Breath and wind, speaking and hearing:
the most natural ways to begin the process.

III.

Waking and Sleeping

WAKING

Breathing, we sleep, and breathing, we awaken.
But how do you wake up in the morning? Take a few moments to analyze the process.
Is there a customary time, and is it maybe a little more relaxed
on weekends?
Is it easy for you to wake up?
What's your usual mood?
What assists do you require—alarm clock, coffee, other regimens
to help you to become fully awake?
Once you are up and about, do you stay relatively awake throughout the day?
A Zen approach may help you to become *alert, alive, aware, awake.*
Try those four *A's* on for size, and see if they describe your general attitude.

Contrasting with those might be *apathy, lethargy,* and *boredom.*

Which of these sets is more characteristically descriptive of who you are?

Have you ever seen a bored squirrel?

That's kind of hard to imagine, and we think instead of the cliché

"bright-eyed, bushy-tailed," or perhaps wired, perpetually on point.

The Nobel laureate Derek Walcott, in *Hymns for the Indigo Hour,*

plays with the image, too, and observes that squirrels "spring up like questions,"

and then again, later: "Squirrels abound, and repeat themselves like questions."

So, ask again my "bored squirrel" question.

And then leave the image, but stay with the word,

boredom.

If Zen were to talk about sin (it doesn't much),

it might isolate boredom as the cardinal sin in life.

There is so much in the created order, in the nature of things,

to make you become vibrantly and radiantly alive—

and you're bored?

The noted Japanese Christian leader Toyohiko Kagawa, more than half a century ago,

penned a prayer which, in its concise eloquence, speaks with the force of a *haiku:*

"May I never find myself yawning at life."

That, indeed, would seem to isolate boredom as the cardinal sin.

A particular *koan* might be a theme for this chapter, as taken from a classic collection,

The Mummonkan:

"Look! The world is vast and wide.

Why do you put on your priest's robe at the sound of a bell?"

Initially, it's simply a wake-up call.

Think of all the incredible number of stimuli that might wake you

from your state of torpor, or sloth!

You're bored? Really?

If you are sensitized to your own need for enlightenment,

imagine an entire nation being aware of that need.

The national anthem of Romania begins with the words

"Wake up, Romanians, from your deathly sleep!"

What if this truly were the consciousness of every nation state—

a widespread earthly reveille?

Do we all need a new level of heightened awareness?

It's *your* personal wake-up call as well!

It's your bell, your signal, your alarm clock

that reminds you each morning that there are tasks to perform,

a role to fulfill, your equivalent of the priest's robe to put on—

We're not talking here in cosmic terms, of *Enlightenment,*

or the Zen heroic breakthrough moments called *kensho,* or *satori.*

Satori is closely related to the words *kaku* and *sameru,*

which have the common meaning "to wake up,"

And again, the word *buddha* simply means "One who woke up!"

The man whom we call The Buddha taught that each of us has a nature

that is wake-up-able!

And maybe those little awakenings are keys to larger ones.

Maybe it does matter just how you wake up each morning.

Do you really need the sound of a bell to get you to put on your priest's robe?

Do you actually require that external signal that you've programmed?

Zen counsels us, very simply, very obviously,

"If you are hungry, eat;

if you are sleepy, sleep."

So, what's the parallel insight for your daily arousal?

We have to coin a word for this:

"If you're awake, awake"

Can you really trust yourself to rise by your own internal rhythms?
You've had nightmares about missing signals, being late for important engagements,
rising from sound slumber, alarmed, because you haven't heard the alarm,
and meanwhile, your priest's robe is languishing on the bedpost,
and you've blown it.
For some of us, that's about as threatening as nightmares get—
unprepared—no priest's robe,
or whatever clothing you don, equipment you require, or work you need to do
to fulfill the tasks of your profession.

There are two Greek words for time,
kronos, which is measurable, clock time,
And *kairos,* which has the sense of timing,
fitting the action to the opportunity, an idea whose time has come.
That's the only word, *kairos,* that really matters; *kronos* is a fiction:

THERE IS NO COSMIC CLOCK!!
(Is that what Einstein meant by relativity?)

No cosmic clock, and all the other clocks, or bells,
that summon us, that inform or alarm us,
are only tools of convenience that regiment us
but may impair our genuine experience of an internal timing (not time) table.
If you've cultivated a *kairos* table,
it might mean that you have so completely ingested your assumed tasks into your psyche,
letting them infiltrate into your subconscious,
informing your waking/sleeping cycle, that you can genuinely say

"Now I lay me down to sleep"
in quietness and in confidence.
"And when I am *awaky*, I will awake!
I won't blow it; I'll awake when I need to!"
You take your rest, knowing that you will, in the sense of *kairos*,
the fullness of time, your time, be *awaky*,
and that you can genuinely look forward to arising.

What would give you that pleasant sensation?
Maybe just knowing that the morning paper awaits you,
or consciously cuddling, for a few moments, the one beside you,
or the prospect of enjoying a leisurely breakfast,
or simply thinking of all that will command your attention in the coming day,
in donning your priest's robe,
that and all the non-role-prescribed joys and surprises
that you may, with assurance, anticipate?
Maybe the prospect of some or all of these might trigger for you a happy smile,
and that first conscious breath which opens your mouth into a wide yawn
(This is a different yawn, you'll notice, from boredom's yawn;
with this one you inhale the morning in lungsful of welcoming air!),
and on arising, that pleasant widening and elongating stretch which reaches out
to touch the world.

A friend of mine, Francis Ormiston, does it even better.
I first met him more than forty years ago and was quickly impressed
by his vital, high energy, his charismatic presence
that would lift the level of intensity in a room when he would enter.
His wife told me how he'd wake up in the morning.

After those first few moments of coming into focus,
he would roll back in the bed, his legs up, and then *vault* out of bed,
almost literally hitting the ground running!
Your style and mine are doubtless a little more gentle,
and his wife tells me that now, in his seventies, he's slowed down a little, too,
but imagine it, waking in that spirit—
What would it be like?
A young Canadian Inuit poet, Panegoosho, says,
"I wake with morning yawning in my mouth."
Those morning moments may persist, and color the whole of your day with joy.
Consider again what each day may offer you.

Long before Zen practices ripened,
there was a Buddhist formula that speaks to this theme:
"Nirvana = Samsara"
Nirvana has been described as a kind of goal-less goal.
It does not feed ego-driven ambition.
It really means a kind of snuffing out, or a transcending, of the ego.
Not much to look forward to here!
And the companion, *Samsara,* underscores the truth of Nirvana,
for *Samsara* means the sea of change, or the world as it is.
So the formula could be translated,
THIS IS IT!!
Right now—not in some other place or time, but
right now, right here, where you are,
THIS IS IT!!
And your first response, as a thoroughly enculturated Westerner, is to feel cheated:
"You mean, *THIS* is it??"

And you think of all the things missing from your scene—
things that don't seem quite ideal—
Maybe you're having financial trouble,
or relationships aren't quite in order,
or your children aren't behaving very well,
or things seem generally too chaotic,
or life just doesn't seem very satisfying,
And now you read, *"THIS IS IT!!?"*
"I thought that religion was supposed to give me the prospect of something better!"
And often it has.
Think of all the things that religions have offered as compensation
for the barrenness of the present, all the fantasied futures,
the utopias, the Elysian fields, the visions of Paradise.
And the Buddhist promise is just
THIS IS IT!!??

That sounds like a hope that's no hope. Right. Feel the radical character of it.
You are simply offered *NOW:* total immersion in this moment,
this day, with no escape clauses.
Recall the image of the digital watch from the previous chapter,
and get the challenge of it:
Whatever else there is, or was, or might be, you have this day.
Can you match the gift with your highest attention and appreciation?
Can you feel the possibilities resident within it?

SLEEPING

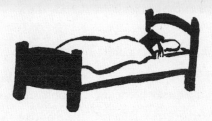

And then, continuing the theme, can you, at the day's close,
in serenity of spirit, lay it all aside, good, bad and indifferent, and
"Lie down to pleasant dreams"?
Ah, but your response may dismiss that image:
"Romantic balderdash! My days end," you may say,
"with the consciousness of unfinished business, frustrations, deadlines missed,
and the certainty that worry about tomorrow's crowded agenda
will keep me tossing and turning all night!
Lie down to pleasant dreams? Sure. And if you tell me
This is it,
then, waking or sleeping, day in, day out, I'm really missing something."
That may be possible. But stay with the feeling. Intensify it.
Hear the world's greatest sleep-cynic, Macbeth, observe,
certainly from his own experience,
that "Wicked dreams abuse the curtain'd sleep."
And then he hears a voice cry, *"Sleep no more! Macbeth does murder sleep."*
What murders sleep for you?
If not a terrible troubled conscience like Macbeth's, then what?

Nudgings of conscience, perhaps?
A word spoken carelessly, something you forgot to do,
a strained friendship, an embarrassing *faux pas*—
a fresh concern with a child or an aging parent,
and you can't quite let it go; sleep is elusive.

Or maybe the situation's more chronic, a problem that you can never quite resolve,
and in the watches of the night it assumes elephantine proportions.
You're worried that you're becoming a full-blown insomniac.
And, like Macbeth, you long for "the innocent sleep;
Sleep that knits up the ravell'd sleave of care,
The death of each day's life, sore labour's bath,
Balm of hurt minds, great nature's second course,
Chief nourisher in life's feast."
And maybe you hear the same voice which haunted him:
"Macbeth shall sleep no more."

Heavy. Too heavy, I hope. You probably don't feel that desperate.
But there are still times when you wish you could turn off your mental motor.
You try all the sleep strategies, and maybe somewhere, in the back of your mind,
you recall a pop song that Eddie Fisher sang decades ago:
"If you're worried, and you can't sleep,
Just count your blessings instead of sheep,
And you'll go to sleep counting your blessings."

Good counsel.
Perhaps you recall making such lists at bedtime as a child,
lists of blessings or thank-yous that grew longer, compulsively,
not as sleep but as stalling strategies, to postpone the inevitable!

You weren't quite ready to let go of the day.
But now you are, and your mind isn't!
You are at cross-purposes with your mind,
and you think of all the ways to find that cut-off switch,
forcefully saying, "Down, boy!"
But the mind's rebellious.
You try to persuade it, rationally:
"I need my eight hours! I'll be a wreck tomorrow!"
Talk about self-fulfilling prophecies: Tomorrow, you are!
Victimized by some pervasive strain of dogmatism that has persuaded us,
collectively, that we need *eight* hours of sleep each night!
Maybe you've modified the time a little, and made it still more generous—
ten, in your case.
Or maybe you've read, as I have, that intelligent people need less sleep.
So you try to do with *seven* hours, or *six*, proving the point.
But it's still a rigid quota that becomes self-defeating.
Our sleep patterns are so infinitely varied.

Mathew Brady once did some classic Civil War photographs,
and one is of a trench outside Petersburg, Virginia,
filled with Confederate dead.
Brady made an accompanying observation:
"No two men have fallen in the same position."
The same is true of our sleep styles, too.
Not just our positions, and our strange habits
of flopping back and forth between them.
Maybe you doze off for a while late in the evening,
and then rouse yourself to go to bed;
maybe you wake, troubled, far too early.

45

"Shall I get up? Shall I stay here and keep fighting?"
And it's so hard simply to accept that, on a given night,
your mind has better things to do than sleep.

Don't call it insomnia; call it *meditation!*
That gets you off the hook of thinking you're sick.
Follow the train of thought that has awakened you,
instead of hassling your mind.
There's another agenda that your deeper recesses insist on,
giving them precedence over the rhythms
that your conscious "priestly-robed" identity wants to impose!
It does indeed impose.
It imposes *kronos,* clock-time, on your sleep schedule
as well as your waking schedule!
And the internal rhythms, which vary nightly, are violated.

Instead of concerns with time, just settle into the quiet emptiness
of the beautiful, mysterious night.
You don't have to fill it; let it fill you.
Hear the lucid imagery of Dogen's *haiku:*
"Midnight. No waves,
no wind, the empty boat
is flooded with moonlight."
Your mind's boat, so flooded, may sink into the deepest tranquility.

Or is it dreams, or the fear of them, that disturb your slumber?
Recurrent nightmares, or weird, troubling ones
that don't make any sense, but bother you on awaking.
You try to dismiss them, but they nag at you,

and in at night, at bedtime,
your worries of more such dreams again trouble your sleep.
The fear of interrupted sleep has robbed us
of what Erich Fromm once called "the forgotten language," the language of dreams.
So-called primitives know that language.
We have reports that tribes like the Senoi in Malaysia
often use the breakfast table as a dream clinic,
detoxifying the fears, domesticating the monsters,
recovering the positive wisdom that comes in our dreams.

Carl Jung, in the same vein, once interviewed a medicine man in Africa
who complained of being underemployed.
Since the white man had come, he lamented, nobody dreamed anymore.
Dreams were an obvious diagnostic tool for him,
but the white man's "rationality" had truncated the people's collective psyche,
so that truths emanating from deeper recesses now were seen as inconsequential.
Again, dreams, the forgotten language.

Have you ever kept a dream diary?
Have you ever paid enough attention to your dreams that you can count on them,
and anticipate their quite regular appearance?
"I wonder what's playing on the late show tonight?"
Your dreams can genuinely offer entertainment as well as learning value.

Trust them. Employ a Little Bo-Peep strategy with them:
"Leave them alone, and they'll come home."
You could, of course, like the overzealous shepherd,
go out and hassle your troubling dreams,
and bring them home.

But they won't be "wagging their tails behind them,"
delighted with the prospect of teaching you
what they've learned from their romps in the midnight meadows.
Learn the Taoist lesson of *wu-wei*, non-intrusive action.
Or as Shunryu Suzuki counsels us:
"To give your sheep or cow a large spacious meadow
is the way to control him."
Or maybe better, speaking of our dreams, it's the way to liberate them.

There are ways of recovering Fromm's lost language.
Begin just by paying attention,
welcoming your dreams, learning from them.
Perhaps Paul Valéry's counsel is applicable:
"The best way to make your dreams come true is to wake up."

WAKING AND SLEEPING

In Japan, the butterfly often appears as the image conjured by poets
when they want to convey that fragile passage between waking and sleeping.
Thus Chuang Tzu in China, whose dream of being a butterfly confused him:
"Was he a man dreaming of being a butterfly,
or a butterfly dreaming of being a man?"
The butterfly became his lifelong reflective companion.
So too with Lafcadio Hearn, who came to Japan in 1890 as a young man.
He stayed there for the rest of his life, and recorded three butterfly *haiku*
that invite the reader to ruminate on the waking-sleeping connection.
In translation the first one reads:

"Perched upon the temple bell,
The butterfly sleeps."
(Consider it: The temple bell gives those "priest robe" signals!
But the butterfly is undisturbed by the threat of that deafening "BONG!"
and actually sleeps there!)

The second:
"Even while sleeping,
Its dream is of play—
Ah, the butterfly of the grass!"
Hearn comments, "Even while it is resting,
the wings of the butterfly may be seen to quiver at moments—
as if the creature were dreaming of flight."

And the third:
"Wake up! wake up!—
I will make thee my comrade,
Thou sleeping butterfly."
(As did Chuang Tzu: See Professor Wu's *The Butterfly as Companion*,
which contains meditations on Chuang Tzu.)
The last *haiku*, Hearn notes, is by the greatest *haiku* composer, Basho,
and it is intended to convey the joyous feeling of springtime.

Perhaps, then, you can create a butterfly bridge,
gracefully, gratefully, moving between the realms of waking and sleeping,
beyond the intruding bells that so often produce such unnatural,
imposed rhythms on your life.

IV.
MOVING AND STAYING

On waking, we begin to move; sleeping, we settle in, stay.
But our moving may be walking in place, marking time,
and sleeping may transport us to other realms!

It's difficult to know which is which,
and which of them, moving or staying, comes first.
We're always playing that familiar chicken-and-egg game.

In Japan, they serve a dish called oya-ko donburi,

or simply *oya-ko don.*

Donburi refers just to the rice that accompanies so many dishes.

Oya-ko means "parent-child," and it's a chicken-and-egg dish!

So you're invited to play a philosophical game with your meal, and to ask,

"Which is which, parent or child?"

"Which came first, the chicken or the egg?"

And for our purposes, which comes first, moving or staying?

It seems as if staying would,

but maybe the question is moot.

The cosmos is full of both gravity and motion,

in constant vacillation.

Einstein again: no cosmic clock regulates the alternating current between the two;

once more, it's relativity, and that implies *kairos:* timing.

Your role and mine is to harmonize with the timing around us,

finding our own fulfillment and psychic balance.

Zen, I think, can help us with that balance.

The Chinese Zen master Linji (called Rinzai in Japanese), once said:

"If you try to grasp Zen in movement, it goes into stillness.

If you try to grasp Zen in stillness, it goes into movement.

It is like a fish hidden in a spring,

drumming up waves and dancing independently.

Movement and stillness are two states.

The Zen master, who does not depend on anything,

makes deliberate use of both movement and stillness."

The Zen master's counsel is present even if the master is absent.

You are given leave, then, like the hidden fish,

to do your own drumming up of waves and independent dancing,

and to return, by your timetable, to the springs that sustain you.

Do your own *zenning*, then; meditate with me on movement and stillness.

You and I will be deliciously refreshed,

as fishes nourished in dancing waves, by this *oya-ko donburi* dish!

There are abundant spiritual linkages between the themes of moving and staying.

Think of how the great religious traditions, relatively stable in themselves,

have spawned so many movements:

movements, of course, of spiritual renewal

or even revolution in their radical character;

movements of social justice, enlisting vast multitudes in marches.

We think of Gandhi's Salt March in India,

or the civil rights marches led by Martin Luther King.

Have you ever been part of such a march or cause

that compelled you to take a visible, public stance?

The impulse may have seemed, at the time, a passing fad,

or something just made you want to get on the bandwagon.

But maybe it had more substance than that.

Maybe it was dictated by your deepest religious convictions,

those most stable values which motivated your action.

Perhaps it has had lasting character.

You may have learned how to channel

moral fervor in a moment into

moral fiber in a movement.

You were not simply caught up in a wave of enthusiasm;

you geared your energies to a long-term commitment.

You stayed in a movement: moving and staying.

Or think of *pilgrimage.*

Pilgrimage involves the movement of people to a place that is stable,
a place of sacred repose, hallowed by what it has preserved,
a fixed place that generates traffic toward it.
Mecca, Benares, Rome, Lourdes, Jerusalem, Sarnath—
these and other myriad holy sites of all the religions of the world.
Some may have inspired your own pilgrimage,
and in addition to such commonly recognized sacred spaces,
you will have your own special spots,
places hallowed by family associations, homesteads,
places where you and your parents lived before,
places where your children live now, places where you attended school.
It is more than the indulgence of nostalgia to visit them.
You walk through a cemetery, stopping by a particular grave,
remembering, and leaving flowers, perhaps.
You drive, you walk, and then you stop.
You can't stay, but you go from wherever you are now living
to stop briefly where a cherished one abides, always.

Moving and staying.

And it isn't morbid to remind yourself that your own short pauses now,
interruptions in what often seems a too-frenetic pace,
characterized only by motion, that these are but waystations,
predictive of that time when others will pause above your own still life.
Or consider the holidays that set you in motion:
Christmas: maybe the star didn't move,
but it set people in motion, and still it does.
Or Thanksgiving: imaginatively, you go to Plymouth,
a place of national beginnings, as you gather around a family table.

It's hard to imagine one of these holidays
when you would not want to host or attend a celebration
with those dear to you.
There is something stable in that,
and you are moved to join that familiar feast once more.

And consider the *moving* and *staying* in your psychic rhythms.
Wordsworth once defined poetry as "emotion reflected in tranquility."
So the alternation of emotion, (e-*motion*, or psychic motion),
with moments of stillness, pondering,
defines the course of our lives as spiritual beings.
Intensity of feeling, and times of cultivated quietness.

Zen, in the concept of mindfulness, gently nudges us to bring these two realms,
moving and staying,
together, internally and externally.
Stillness in the midst of activity,
awareness brought to immediate focus on whatever you're doing,

That's the ideal.
It can become the practice.
Try it with walking,
our most natural, non-vehicular, and thus non-violent form of locomotion.

A couple of years ago I took a walk with Rudy Mancke,
producer/director of *NatureScene,*
a nationally distributed educational television series.
Our group walked for an hour;
I could have covered ten times the distance in that time,

and totally missed what the walk offered.
He gave me the chance to see with his naturalist's, or maybe with Zen, eyes.
Seeing, then stopping, then the quick swish of Mancke's butterfly net,
and, after careful extraction,
a close encounter with a dragonfly, then a butterfly,
shared with the small group.
Still closer with the aid of a magnifying glass—
the visage, at that range, looks pretty fearsome!
It was a different way of walking—and seeing.
Sometimes I join my wife in power-walking;
we get some good exercise.
"Feel the swinging of your arms, your lengthened, accelerated stride,
your stepped-up rate of breathing."
It can be exhilarating!

But I prefer *sauntering*.
Henry David Thoreau, who must have practiced it a lot,
reminds us that the word may have a double derivation.
Saunterer may come from the designation applied in the Middle Ages
to one who was bound for the *Sainte Terre*, or Holy Land.
Or it may come from *sans terre*, one who is without a home,
and, as Thoreau notes, is equally at home anywhere.
Both are richly suggestive for our purposes.
The saunterer may regard the very earth on which she walks
as *sainte terre*, holy ground.
She is a gentle crusader,
not like the ones who sought to reconquer the Holy Land from the infidel,
but one who seeks now, for her own consciousness,
or with wider ecological concern,

to return to and reclaim the land for its innate, implicit holiness.

She isn't headed toward some other, more holy ground.

Each step is sacred.

And if she is *sans terre*, without home,

then, as Thoreau suggests, she is at home anywhere.

The wildest scene is not tamed,

but her own domesticated mind-set matches its wildness.

A Sierra Club motto states it: "The world is a wildlife preserve,

and we are the wild-life."

So, put the terms together, incongruously, to form a natural *koan*,

and *cultivate wildness.*

Wildness really is a state of liberation.

You enter the natural state of things, and discover your natural self—

another way to understand what sauntering means.

Kindred words such as *meander* or *wander* can convey it, too.

Conjure the Hindu image of the *sannyasin,* or holy wanderer:

it presents us with the ideal of a path which is no path,

with no destination,

not subject to the normal demands of a householder's existence.

A few years ago, the state of Indiana had a slogan on its license plates—

"Wander Indiana."

Presumably that meant that,

to the person with a refined, subtle aesthetic sensibility,

a drive through Indiana, a state not lavished with dramatic natural attractions,

beauty appears around every corner.

The term *wander* seems to convey an aimless, goal-less journey,

whose rhythms are dictated by an openness to whatever path seems to beckon.

When was the last time that you walked in that frame of mind?
Maybe it was in your own backyard,
just savoring the luxuriant joy of what you'd helped to shape and fashion.
Or maybe it was something much more extravagant,
like hiking in the Himalayas.
I remember my own Himalayan hike: there was a path, and a destination,
but I was by myself, and the time was my own, for three days.
It was an incredibly heady, intoxicating time.
But the time and expense of a Himalayan hike may be wasted
if you haven't cultivated the sheer pleasure of sauntering on familiar turf.
Thoreau knew that, and, as was said of him, he "traveled much in Concord."
Maybe that means that, in his sauntering, each scene was different,
each time he walked his familiar terrain with *seeing* eyes.

Some of your journeys may be solo,
but many will be with familiar companions, or like Dorothy on the way to Oz,
you may pick up some new and fascinating travelers on the road.
Once, studying for a term at Canterbury,
I found sections of the Pilgrims' Way, and walked them one day.
I felt adventurous, but missed Chaucer's colorful characters:
the Clerk, the Widow of Bath. The journey wasn't quite authentic.
Some pilgrimages aren't the same without fellow pilgrims; who are yours?

And what are the other variables, in journeys close or far?
Not the duration or distance,
but the capacity to have your senses activated,
attuned to what is there around you, sharing with those who travel with you,
savoring it all.

Gary Snyder, in *The Practice of the Wild,*
talks about being driven around the Australian bush for a few hours,
and having his driver rapidly relate the stories of the land
through which they were traveling.
One story would end, and, pointing to another place,
the driver would immediately begin another story,
at the same breakneck speed.
Finally, feeling sensory overload,
Snyder realized that these were Dreamtime Stories,
tales of origins, particular to each place,
and meant to be told or sung while strolling.
The topography of these songline maps, passed from generation to generation,
was too detailed for anything but walking.

The land, the *sainte terre,* has stories which can only
be heard at a walking pace.
Walking, and with time allowed for pauses, reflecting—
this lets you catch the alternate rhythms of moving and staying—
and lets the holy land speak to you.
Activate all the senses, experience the sights, the sounds,
the smells, the touch, the taste of the sacred land,
and all that its creatures and contours want to say to you.
Read Frederick Franck's classic book, *The Zen of Seeing.*
Elsewhere Franck recalls his childhood fascination
(which I remember, too) with his parents' stereopticon slides.
A card with two identical pictures, side by side,
was placed in a holder in front of the lenses, cushioned by felt,
against which you placed your eyes.

The miracle then occurred: you saw the image in three dimensions!
The slides we had were of World War I, and many were graphic, even gory.
But reflecting on the magic of the three-dimensional slides,
Franck realized that this is the way that we always see,
in three dimensions,
and when the world of his childhood would seem flat and drab,
he would remind himself, "Use your stereopticon eyes!"
And the magic would return.
If Rabindranath Tagore could say, "My religion is a poet's religion,"
with senses enhanced and language sensitized
to express their fine-tuned messages,
then Franck could say, "My religion is an artist's religion."
In the best fidelity to the spirit of The Buddha,
the one among many enlightened or potentially enlightened beings,
he teaches the reader/seer to glimpse what he sees.
We have stereopticon eyes, too, and we are in that sense artists!
And perhaps he can teach us to draw expressively, also,
transposing the artist's vision to the canvas.
(I'm a little less confident of that—
could he really liberate my own graphically challenged hand?
My eyes, maybe,
but the intimidation factor is even stronger with expressing in pictures
what my eyes see than it is in words.
Which comes easier for you?)

In China the word for landscape is *shan-shui*, which means "mountain-water."
Perhaps you've seen hanging screens depicting vast, mysterious mountains
in the background, with a stream running beneath them,

and perhaps a tiny, hermetic figure by the stream, pondering.
That motif is such a common one in Chinese and Japanese painting,
much of it linked with Zen poetic expression.
Imaginatively, paint yourself into that landscape, as the tiny figure,
dwarfed by the haunting majesty of the mountains
and charmed by the stream which hurries from their recesses.
You are in that scene, with powers of reflection,
expressed in words or brush.
The landscapes around you can speak to your soul in the same way.
The hermit by the mountain stream, like Thoreau, may not travel far,
but staying, he moves with the stream.

SueEllen Campbell, in her book *Bringing the Mountain Home*,
captures the idea:
"I believe the desire for wildness is an elemental force, like gravity,
like magnetism, with the power of a lodestone, a charged center of mass
and energy, a deeply loved landscape holds us fast to the planet."

That's staying, but it's not static.
Wildness energizes us, vitalizes that sleepy core within us, lulled by convention.
But it also grounds us, giving us the sense of cherished space that is home.
Are you considering a move? Or whether you should stay,
in a place, a job, a relationship?
Zen has less to say, I think, about the ethics of such a choice
than about its aesthetics.
How will these possibilities color your life? What sense do you have
of the rhythms, the timing, the balance
of moving and staying?

I an your own deepest root systems, your most cherished values
be transplanted, or would your life wither
if significant change were engaged?

Consider a model, playing on curious coincidence,
that may articulate these two themes
of staying and moving, moving and staying,
in various ways and intensities in all of the world's religions,
and in each of our lives.
Alex Haley wrote the book, *Roots,*
that captured the television audience of the United States in the seventies.
Around the same time, Arthur Hailey wrote a novel, *Wheels,*
about the automotive industry in Detroit.
One may stand for stability, the other for mobility,
in an intriguing symmetry:

A. Haley	*Roots*	Stability
A. Hailey	*Wheels*	Mobility

And then add another, which breaks the symmetry only slightly,
referring to the classic discovery by Edmund Halley:

E. Halley	Comet	Infinity

Or use this graphic form:

Haley	Hailey	Halley
Roots	Wheels	Comet
Stability	Mobility	Infinity

The great religions recognize our need to be grounded, rooted, in place, in family,
in a tradition which nourishes our spirits.
But they also inspire movements which break up the calcified, atrophied conventions
which challenge social injustice
and resonate with our restless need for adventure.
And religions add the realm of infinity to the earthly rhythms of staying and moving.

The Kansas state motto is *Ad Astra per Aspera,*
"To the stars through difficulty."
I also saw those words in an unlikely location far from my native state,
permanently displayed in the front of a university classroom in Odessa,
in the Ukraine!
What did it mean in that setting?
The stars, a comet, reminding us, always, of the infinite—
it must be a universal dimension, beyond geographical or ideological borders.
At times, in many religions, the infinite descends
to the intimate sphere of our planetary life.
This may be by rare, incarnational appearances,
but often the truth of the divine in our midst is a cornerstone teaching.
With Zen, this is so pervasive that the distinction
between the two spheres is blurred, even obliterated.
One may speak of the naturally divine or the fully human interchangeably.
Again, we simply need to awaken to that "more"
dimension that was there, in our life landscapes, all along,
helping us to intuit the passages between them.

Or are they really *Land-Water Scapes?*
Is that the insight of the Zen interpretation of *shan-shui:*

that the borders of land and water,

as with staying and moving,

highlight each other's beauty?

That they belong on the same canvas?

Imagine how my psyche, from its landlocked youth in Kansas,

with few streams and lakes,

sight-seeing and psyche-seeing the ocean for the first time at age sixteen,

would respond to my recent experience of traveling around the world by ship

for a hundred days!

I was teaching in the University of Pittsburgh's Semester at Sea program,

and it was an incredibly rich time for me.

You will doubtless have walked by the seashore,

or perhaps traveled on the ocean's surface, much sooner than I.

And you have known, as Melville spoke of it,

the natural connection between water and meditation.

How could it be otherwise?

Waves, cresting and breaking, surf sounds, the sheer immensity.

Long thoughts: given that immensity, the incredible expanse,

and your own microscopic stature,

the reflective impulse comes unbidden.

Your mind needs no dogmatic, prescribed ordering

to ponder questions that are borderless with mystery:

"Who am I? What is the measure of my days?"

Returning home from my voyage, the pondering continued;

our choral society began rehearsals for a production of Ralph Vaughan Williams,

A Sea Symphony, to the poetry of Walt Whitman.
With the poet, orchestrated by the music, each of us may be moved to say,

"Sailing these seas or on the hills, or waking in the night,
Thoughts, silent thoughts, of Time and Space and Death, like waters flowing,
Bear me indeed as through the regions infinite,
Whose air I breath, whose ripples hear, lave me all over,
Bathe me, O God, in thee, mounting to thee,
I and my soul to range in range of thee."
That's the traveler's voice, and I continue to relive
my own "Sea Symphony," in singing and remembering
impressions that those lines recall,
But hear once more the voice of the consummate stay-at-home traveler,
Thoreau: "There are continents and seas in the moral world,"
he reminds us, "to which every man is an isthmus or an inlet."
From this, he gives us the universal imperative:
"to explore the private sea, the Atlantic and Pacific of one's being alone."

That's the inner task that compels us all.
In your own voyage of discovery
you will know such mandates, and moments such as these,
in the rhythms of your own moving and staying.
They must be pursued, and mindfully nourished, when they come,
so that your spirit is tutored in wonder,
charmed by the possibilities around you and beyond,
and knowing the rightness, for you,
of responding to the urgings of each, as they appear.

V.
EATING AND DRINKING

We wake, we walk, we stay on the move,
and soon enough, we eat and drink.
That's life; that's Zen.
Someone once asked Master Yun-men,
"What is the most urgent phrase?"
The Master said, "Eat!"
That says it simply enough. What's more basic?

Again, to the same point, a monk asked Master Ummon,
"What is that surpasses the Buddhas, surpasses the Patriarchs?"
Ummon replied, "Buns."
Or as Jesus said, "Give us this day our daily buns."

Sort of. In either version, the lesson is the same.
Take it literally: "O taste and see."
Don't simply cogitate about it, eat it! Be consumed by it!
We are delivered from the abstract, the cerebral,
to engage the everyday realities of life.
Senses, not pretenses: this is a pervasive theme of Zen,
and our sensory gifts are subjects for doxologies.

On the top of a can of Van Camp's baked beans I read:
"Shake 'em. Hear how good they taste."
That's synesthesia, the sensory distinctions blurring,
so that we perceive holistically,
and celebrate what we perceive.

DINING DISORDERS

It's so easy to focus on the problems connected with eating and drinking:
gluttony, drunkenness, anorexia, bulimia, being stoned, hooked,
all the ways in which we are obsessed with food and drink.
We are afflicted with "affluenza," addicted to excess,
indicted by our appetites.
Graphic depictions of the faces of the world's hungry millions
sober us, shame us,
as do our own bloated mirror images.
So many items crop up on the "bad for you" list
that food and drink carry with them almost generic poison labels.
Obsession alternates with aversion,

implied in the "food is poison" messages contained in the marketing words
diet, lite, low-cal, no-cal, low-fat, no-fat, healthy (??),
masking plastic low-taste, no-taste products.
Or maybe our penchant for fast foods and "instant" everything
means that we have lost our taste for the artistry
of preparing and enjoying food.
Impatient palates: the pollution of time.
We may subvert the pleasure of conversation, the savoring of food
carefully, lovingly prepared.
There's a Zen proverb that says,
"A superior vessel takes a long time to complete."

Or maybe consumption itself, as well as the time taken for the process,
carries with it overtones of guilt.
And the wisdom of the ancient Epicurean counsel,
"Eat, drink and be merry, for tomorrow we die,"
seems like a sanction for debauchery.
Perhaps we trust another Greek dictum more:
"Nothing in excess."
Buddhism, the Middle Way, would seem generally
to accord well with that.

SENSORY CELEBRATION

Zen, however, seems less fearful of excess,
and appears to talk more of celebration than moderation.
For all its strenuous disciplines,

Zen is still replete with profligates and prodigals
who never came home, who remained always
wastrel wanderers, careless of conventions,
winers and diners at the world's trough (not table),
intoxicant inebriates of life.
Zen treasures its iconoclasts, like Ikkyu.

Offered an abbacy in a subtemple of the Daitokuji monastery
in Kyoto in the fifteenth century, he resigned in less than two weeks,
leaving this testament:
"Only ten fussy days as an abbot
And already my feet are tangled in red tape.
If, someday, you want to look me up,
try the fish-shop, the tavern, or the brothel."
You get the feeling that Ikkyu was not a connoisseur of haute cuisine
but a slurper of rough but robust fare in bawdy dens.
Ikkyu is not alone. Zen painters adopted other rogue figures
as models for Zen masters and monks,
such as the crazy hermits Han-shan and Shih-te,
and the laughing, strangely adorably fat Pu-tai.
You can't gaze at him without smiling.
His image is affirmed from another source, a passage from the Hebrew Bible,
where the prophet known as Second Isaiah exhorts his hearers:
"Eat what is good, and delight yourselves in fatness."

That sounds so out of sync with the sleek, svelte image
that you and I want to project,
but at least listen to the validation of natural, joyful appetites which it conveys.

Neither advertisers of lite products, nor nutritionists, nor puritans,
can measure the sheer aesthetic pleasure,
the life-enhancement that eating and drinking provide.

A MATTER OF TASTE

"Is it good for you?"
"Do you enjoy it?"
Each question is legitimate,
the first asking you to assess nutritional value,
but the second, in accord with the Zen spirit,
asking you to enjoy taste, to dwell sensually within it,
and that's very much a personal matter.

The Latin proverb says it: *"De gustabis non est disputandem"*:
"There's no quarreling with taste."
It isn't just a question of having "good taste."
Your preferences, strange as they may appear to me,
do not need to audition for legitimacy
before some taste tribunal.
So—what particular foods, and accompanying settings,
stimulate your salivation?
(A bizarre religion: is Zen more concerned with salivation than salvation?)
Are there any consensual delectables?

Try *chocolate.* Or *pizza.*
Or one of a host of favorite ethnic foods; check your response to each:

Mexican, Greek, Italian, Chinese,
German, Indian, Arabic, French,
Japanese, Thai, African—
(Are all of these really soul food?)
You have, like the rest of us, about ten thousand taste buds;
how many of your ten thousand
are triggered to attention by each of the above, and in what ways?
And do you find that your spirit,
not just your belly and body,
is nourished by this sensory feast?

Try yet another genre: *think Hawaiian!*
A rare tropical blend of many cultures and cuisines:
everything imported, flora and fauna alike,
from the first Polynesians
to generous portions Asian and Caucasian,
flowing together in a mellifluous mix,
and spawning, in Hawaii's unlikely volcanic soil,
mangoes, papayas, coconuts, bananas,
pineapples, avocados, macadamia nuts!
Such incredibly succulent fare,
and you don't have to create a full-blown luau
to savor these delights.
(*Poi,* the native Hawaiian product of the taro root,
would also be on the luau menu,
but most non-native palates won't take to it.)

So, paradoxically, while Buddhism has as a cardinal goal
the reduction of desire,

Zen, simply stated, whets your appetite
for a host of things,
beginning with staple fare, of course, the basics.
Second Isaiah again: "Why do you hunger for that which is not bread,
and your labor for that which does not satisfy?"
It isn't exactly a gourmand's counsel,
or the invitation to a king's lavish banquet,
but it speaks of the nourishment that simple, plebeian pleasures provide.

Or try the Psalmist's incredible assertion:
"He satisfies the desire of every living thing."
Into the fabric of all life this promise,
that for every need that rises from the depth of our nature
there is a means of gratification.
The prophecy seems, however, to beg the insertion of adjectives:
"He satisfies the legitimate, or appropriate, desire . . . ,"
not just the sanctioning of any wish
born of insatiable greed,
but the promise of fulfillment to each natural appetite.
A modern translation of Jesus' words of assurance
from the Sermon on the Mount underscores the promise:
"Beneath the spreading heavens no creature but is fed,
and He who feeds the ravens will give His children bread."

Visualize the same insight in another incredible Zen moment
from Nikos Kazantzakis's *Zorba the Greek*,
where the Boss, the narrator, says,
"I calmly chewed my food in the sun and felt a deep physical happiness
as if I was floating on the cool, green waters of the sea.

I did not allow my mind to take possession of this carnal joy,
to press it into its own moulds, and make thoughts of it.
I let my whole body rejoice from head to foot, like an animal.
Now and then, nevertheless, in ecstasy, I gazed about me and within me,
at the miracle of this life.
What is happening? I said to myself.
How did it come about that the world is so perfectly adapted
to our feet and hands and bellies?
And once again I closed my eyes and was silent."
Savor that scene with me.

Or try yet another, which supplements it, from the film *Babette's Feast.*
Babette, the refugee, who fits so naturally into the spare, Spartan life
of the rural, self-denying Danish religious community,
but who has yet another gift to give, in a lavish feast,
awakening all the dormant taste buds of these frugal folk.
Our daily bread may indeed be frugal,
but it doesn't have to be boring, and occasional forays
into exotic cuisine add spice and zest to our customary fare.
The experience is available,
much more than for the eighteenth-century free-trade advocate who exulted,
"By this we taste the spices of Arabia,
and never feel the scorching heat that brings them forth."
We don't have to cross the desert; they're brought to our doorstep.
The exotic products and their pleasures, like Zen, are portable.
But if you get to sample the original setting,
exotic or otherwise,
or if you cultivate a fertile imagination for it,
then the pleasure is intensified.

Gather macadamia nuts or fruits, then, with me, at a bed-and-breakfast farm,
or at a Buddhist retreat center on Hawaii, the Big Island.
You don't pick the mac nuts from the tree;
when they're ripe, they fall. You gather them.
The macadamia is, literally, a tough nut to crack.
The rough outer shell isn't hard to remove,
but the smooth, inner one is a challenge.
Try to break it with pliers or a normal nutcracker
and you'll probably be frustrated.
But hold it with those same pliers on concrete,
and crack it with a hammer.
Small reward for serious effort? Maybe not.
The focused attention may feel like a Zen tool
that helps you with other tough nuts.

Then, as you break them, one by one, share them, convivially, with others,
like "chestnuts roasting by an open fire"
or walnuts cracked around a table for Christmas cookies.
Delectables. So many rich items on the platter.

EATING, DRINKING AS CONVIVIAL PLEASURE

Sitting by yourself in a crowded restaurant,
or drinking alone at home:
these aren't, for most of us, pleasant images.
And the nutcracking scenes remind us of how much our companions
enrich our wining and dining.

Think of your associations with the phrase "homemade ice cream":
a warm summer evening, a family gathered,
getting out the churn, preparing the mix
(What was your favorite flavor?),
packing the ice and salt around the cylinder,
taking turns, several of you, at the handle,
maybe with someone sitting on a burlap bag on the churn
to keep the whole thing from turning when the mixture began to harden.
And then, when the ice cream was ready, unpacking it, taking it inside,
scooping out the delicious cool, creamy blend
into large bowls, with all the convivial sharing
that a loving family knows. Treasured moments.

Have we missed something?
Have we traded the gustatory delights of homemade ice cream
for Joni Mitchell's "ice cream castles in the air"?
Instead of the genuine nostalgia for moments rich with reality,
is it, again in the words of the popular song,
"life's illusions" we "recall"
and not the bonding feasts nearly buried in memory's long corridors?
Hopefully, you habitually renew, in daily meals, if not in feasts,
the pleasure of those moments with family and friends.
And occasionally you may enjoy the strong stimulation
of an intellectual smorgasbord, like the one in the movie *My Dinner with André*,
each person present intoxicated with ideas
from the sparks struck by the almost electrical exchange.

But in such a heady atmosphere as this,
the food and drink may seem merely a medium for psychic ferment.

Recognizing that, Zen centers, like many other monastic communities,
will regularly, or on occasion, dine in silence,
facilitating a direct experience of the food and drink
without the distraction of conversation.
You may learn to appreciate that, but as a novice,
it will almost certainly feel awkward and unnatural.
But the novice status, as we know from *Zen Mind, Beginner's Mind*,
can be useful in many ways.

Intensify it, by returning to a parent-child role of earlier days.
Think of this as an exercise in experiencing
the *oya-ko* relationship described in the previous chapter.
You will need a partner.
Seat yourselves, facing each other, at the corner of a table,
with your meal before you.
And then, taking turns, bite by bite,
feed each other.
You feed your partner from his/her plate, and vice versa,
offering, as needed,
to raise the other's cup or glass, also.
Do this silently,
and rich non-verbal communication, quite possibly humorous,
should ensue.
You will not remember being fed this way,
but you may remember feeding another.
Your mouth opens in simulation;
you may miss your target a little
and have to use a spoon or fork to clean your partner's lips.
You're a beginner at this;

you may feel playful, even ludicrous.
How does that feel?
Feeding each other will probably take twice the time, surprisingly,
it does to feed yourself.
What do you learn from it?
(Consider it an alternative experience
of the social character of dining.)

Meditate on the themes of emptiness and fullness
before and after your meals.
Emptiness, or *sunyata*, is richly evocative in Buddhism.
Think of it as nothing, or better, no-thing.
Not thinkable, not thing-able,
the void of pure possibility,
ANYTHING!
And if you trust the chef, that's a great setting for a meal:
"Surprise me!"

The parallel to *sunyata*, emptiness,
is *purna*, or fullness.
Couple it with the word *anna*, which means matter, or food,
and you get *Annapurna*, the name of the majestic Himalayan peak,
which might be translated "mass of matter," or better,
like the chain of restaurants in India
named Annapurna, "full of food"!
Emptiness and fullness, hunger and satisfaction:
natural themes for Zen (meditation).

DRINKING

The consummate model in Japan is, of course,
chado, or *cha-no-yu,* the way of tea.
D. T. Suzuki, who is authoritative on so many matters related to Zen,
suggests that tea is for Buddhism what wine is for Christianity.
Each is powerfully symbolic for its tradition,
and each is ritually significant.
The tea ceremony would carry for Zen something akin
to the sacramental intensity of the Eucharist.
It seeks to embody simplicity, even poverty,
actualizing the ideal of the Japanese term *wabi,*
which has been defined as
"not to be in the fashionable society of the time."
Envision, then, a rustic hut,

and a room no larger than ten feet square—
a scene far removed from the gaudiness and fashion of court ritual.
A teamaster may preside as host,
yet this is not hierarchical, but the most democratizing
of arrangements. Distinctions between host and guest
soon dissolve in the commonality of sharing.
The light is dim, encouraging one's vision to turn inward.
Harmony, reverence, purity, and serenity:
as these ideals emerge for persons present,
cha-no-yu becomes indeed an art form.
Tea keeps the mind fresh and alert,
but, unlike wine, it does not intoxicate,
and is thus removed from dangers of excess, in secular settings.
It is closer to nature than culture.
Its "cultivation," consumption, and quiet celebration
are those of a common and not a fine art.
Liken it to a pair of hikers who stoop, cupping their hands
for the refreshing water of a clear mountain stream.
Or think of the wholesome "milk mustache."
That's the clean, pure image of *cha-no-yu*.

It's the same Ikkyu who, as one of the primary transmitters
of the technique of tea, asked his friends,
when he left the monastery, to look for him in the tavern!
Could that setting for him, or our own institution of the happy hour,
or a convivial evening in an English pub,
serve us as a similar secular sacrament?
It isn't just the beverage of choice

but the quality of the occasion, which determines its worth.
Is it life-enhancing, does it deepen relationships?
Is your heart warmed when you leave the company of your friends?
Do you awaken the next morning feeling refreshed? Renewed?

If wine serves a function for Christianity
similar to that of tea for Buddhism,
then coffee would be the Western secular equivalent to tea for the East.
Do you remember your first taste of coffee as a child?
Mine was traumatic.
Intrigued by watching my father's enjoyment of his morning cup of coffee,
I asked for a sip. Black, unsweetened, it tasted horrible!
But, despite the strong aversion, I remember saying,
"I hope I like it when I grow up."
And sure enough, while it's not a regular thing, sometimes I do!
The morning cup or cups, the coffee break, the coffee bar—
while they don't have the same ceremonial or near sacral sense
as does *cha-no-yu*, the tea ceremony,
they still may evoke pleasurable associations.
For me, the early trauma may have left its impress;
sugar and milk are required.
But I am intrigued by all of the varieties and combinations
that have expanded our taste for coffee and its near relations
like espresso, cappuccino, mocha, and hot chocolate!
Read a sampling of menu items from a favorite local coffee and sandwich bar.
(You will have similar fare from some such place in your own locale.)
Cafe au Lait, Cocoa Loco (a mixture of *Dutch Hot Chocolate* and freshly brewed coffee),
Coffee of the Day, and *Iced Coffee of the Day*,

along with *Iced Latte, Iced Mocha,* and *Chococcino.*
The last tastes like a chocolate coffee milkshake,
and the owners swear it's low-fat!
But its high-taste quality is attested by its having spawned
two new varieties, *Espresso Chococcino* and *Mint Chococcino!*
Exotic, yet common delights such as these may be more provocative for your palate
than rare samplings from "casks of amontillado" or vintage champagnes.

Varieties of originals may tempt us,
but in other ways we exhibit an intense orthodoxy of taste.
You will remember the intense promotion of New Coke back in the eighties,
and the equally intense public rejection of it,
so that when the original quickly appeared as an alternative,
marketed now as *Classic,*
the *New* variety moved into total eclipse.
How could you tamper with a product promoted with the words
COKE IS!!
They make it sound as if it's the essence of Being Itself!
Or you may recall the scene of a host of people on a hillside,
merrily singing *"It's the real thing!"*
Again, it's almost a claim for ultimacy.

Pepsi doubtless profited from the Coke wars,
countering with an appeal to timeliness rather than the timeless,
making its pitch to *The NOW Generation* (that almost sounds Buddhist!),
and identifying it as *The Pepsi Generation.*
Both companies promoted, fashionably, their *diet* and *caffeine free* lines,
and an early Coke product, Fresca, with its clean, pure taste,

is released for some of its share the battles

and captures a small share of the market,

by being a *diet* product, and having a tiny proportion of real citrus juice!

And juices themselves, with a perennial appeal,

hold a stable share of the market for predictable health reasons.

Exotic blends intrigue us, and one company promotes them

with an almost sacrilegious pitch:

"Flavors Mother Nature never intended!"

The tempting lure of the ancient Garden to sell a modern product:

Are you supposed to feel a little naughty drinking fruit juice?

SANCTIFIED APPETITES

Beyond the commercial promotions, what remains?

If we cannot quite duplicate the ritual atmosphere of *cha-no-yu*,

Zen's reflective spirit may engage our alerted taste buds, East or West,

with heightened awareness and appreciation,

even a joyful abandonment,

savoring each morsel or drop that passes our lips,

enlarging our appetite for the world's widespread board,

but also making us connoisseurs of the common.

VI.
PLAYING AND WORKING

PLAYING

We've been wined and dined; now we're ready to play, or work!
But what is this?
What's *playing* doing coming before *working*?
Playing is what responsible people do
after they've completed their work.

Everybody knows that.

Well, everybody, maybe, except children,

and a few people who have caught the spirit of Zen.

We begin our lives as *Homo ludens,* defined precisely as being human

by our capacity to play.

As we mature, that capacity may diminish,

and with it our humanness.

How can it be restored?

Play may be defined as pure celebrative self-expression,

untrammeled by self-consciousness

or behavior in pursuit of some goal.

Catch it in Basho's invitation:

"Look children, hail-stones! Let's rush out!"

Caution would say, "Stay inside; it's dangerous!"

And the obedient child misses the miracle.

Self-consciousness would say, "Adults watch the weather, they don't frolic in it!"

And we stay straight, and crippled.

Goal direction would ask, "What's the point?"

And we're left on the sidelines, unable to justify the act.

But hear a poem by the Zen monk Ryokan, from about two centuries ago:

"Spring come again, after moody wintering indoors,

I left the hermitage with begging bowl.

The village children played in the long-awaited sun.

I bounced ball with them, chanting—

one-two-three-four-five-six-seven.

They bounced while I sang,
They sang while I bounced.
So I've wasted, joyfully,
a whole spring day."

Perhaps that's it—the total abandonment of utility.
Hear it again in Lin Yutang's counsel:
"If you can spend a perfectly useless afternoon
in a perfectly useless manner,
you have learned how to live."
You may have done that recently, but I suspect that few of us
could acknowledge to another, with pure satisfaction,
"I've just wasted a whole afternoon,
I had a lot to do, and I did none of it,
and it was glorious."
Can you even imagine that?

I was once in a session at Esalen where one member of the group
volunteered to be stage center.
This workshop, called "Embodied Gestalt,"
focused on growth through integrating body, mind, and spirit,
and often we started with attention to the body.
The volunteer, my roommate for the workshop,
was asked by Ed Smith, the leader, to identify any particular places where he felt
tension or pain, warmth or cold, pressure,
or any other sensation.
My friend, a large, well-built man,
acknowledged feeling pressure on his shoulders.

You could see it, in the way that he sat on the floor,
hunched over, like the weight of the world was on him.
To intensify the feeling, the leader asked the two largest men in the group
to lean on his shoulders, with their full weight,
and then, after a moment, asked him to see if he could release that burden.
He first simply tried, with all his strength, to rise,
but they were too heavy.
Then he moved adroitly out from under them,
and they fell to the floor.
In the moments that followed the pressures were identified,
the accompanying feelings were accessed,
along with possible ways of dealing with them.
Catharsis and insight seemed genuine,
reinforced by group support.

Maybe if the work load, the pressure, from whatever source
is too heavy, your best strategy is not simply
to summon more energy against it, to work harder,
countering strength with strength.
Try a diversion. Like *play*.
Imagine this scene that a Zen saying conjures:
"How refreshing, the whinny of a packhorse,
unloaded of everything!"
What would that feel like?
Christmas Humphreys, who established the Buddhist Society in London in 1925,
observed, "There is more honest belly laughter in a Zen monastery
than surely in any other religious institution on earth."
But it may not be reserved to Zen.

Why play? Why laugh?
For therapy, for balance, for healing, if it requires justification.
And sometimes we do seem to need to justify it.
Judaism, in exile, asked the pervasive question,
"How do we sing the Lord's song in a strange land?"
And today, how can we, authentically, play or sing
in a world scarred by Auschwitz and My Lai,
and the killing fields of Cambodia and Kosovo?
We are so often in a strange and cruel land,
and anger and lamentation, not belly laughter,
are the appropriate core emotions of the religious life
at century's end, aren't they?

But then there's a sad, gaunt figure from the nineteenth century,
reading the comic poetry of Artemus Ward to his cabinet
in the midst of the Civil War.
You can see their straight spines, their sober faces,
as they waited stiffly for him to finish this frivolity,
which seemed so out of character for him
and so obscene in a time of national calamity.
Abraham Lincoln then asked, "Gentlemen, why don't you laugh?"
It was an indispensable therapy for him.
Norman Cousins discovered, more recently,
the specific healing character of laughter in his own grave illness.

The religious institution and the individual, East or West, need this balance,
and in other times we have known it.
Fasting seems better able to be observed in the church year

when feasting, or carnival, precedes it.
So the medieval church used to satirize itself
in a feast of fools or a donkey festival.
Perhaps Coventry Patmore is right when he speaks of a quality of love
which lifts the spirit above the realms of worship and reverence
into spheres of laughter and dalliance.
That reverses the order, doesn't it?
Laughter is the music of the spheres!
It is the most fervent of prayers, embracing the universe with joy.
It helps us to recover the naturally divine.

Do you recall a moment when you were so doubled up with laughter
that your stomach muscles ached?
Maybe it was contagious, infectious laughter in a group.
What triggered it?
Can you induce that, now, in a few minutes of laughing meditation?
Recapture that moment in its intensity,
or another really funny occasion,
and see if a smile comes naturally, and widens,
and maybe, spontaneously, becomes audible laughter.
Indulge that. It might make things lighter.
Take the world, then, as a heavy burden off the shoulders of Atlas
and make it a small ball, held playfully in the palm of a child's hand.
So, it's time out; let's play. Conjure your childhood.
What associations do you have with words or images like these?
Play-Doh, yo-yo, hula hoop,
slippery-slide, teeter-totter,
running in your backyard with a beloved puppy,

playing in a sandpile, jumping on a bed,

playing hopscotch, throwing a Frisbee,

skipping!

Now tell me, when have you last skipped?

Right now, try it; I just did!

(Imagine me, aging professor, leaving my office, skipping down the hall,

through our secretary Anne's, office, inviting her to join me—

she did!—and back again.)

It was perfectly liberating.

And it might have been even more so

if I had a child, hand in hand, to skip with me.

But my grandkids live out of town! Resolution: *next visit.*

Now try this: for an alternative activity,

access the recesses of your memory and sing along:

"O little playmate,

come out and play with me,

under the apple tree,

and bring your dollies three.

Climb up my rain-barrel,

slide down my cellar-door.

and we'll be jolly friends, forevermore."

Just as Jesus set a child in the midst of his hearers,

so the invitation for us to meet our own forgotten child is perpetually renewed.

How can I play in a strange land?

In spite of everything, we witness the capacity for play, for laughter—

the victories of the spirit.

Several years ago I heard a presentation of *I Never Saw Another Butterfly*,
a musical memorial to the 15,000 children who passed through Theresienstadt
on their way to Auschwitz.
The text is from the poetry of these children,
and the last of nine poems is particularly memorable.
It's titled "Bird Song."
"He doesn't know the world at all,
Who stays in his nest and doesn't go out.
He doesn't know what the birds know best,
Nor what I care to sing about.
That the world is full of loveliness
When the dew drops sparkle in the grass
And earth's a-flood with morning light.
A black bird sings upon a bush
To greet the dawning after night.
Then I know how fine it is to be alive.
Hey, open up your heart to beauty;
Go to the woods some day
And weave a wreath of memory there.
Then, if tears obscure your way
You'll know how wonderful it is
To be alive."

An incredible testimony. It is, of course, the song of the innocents,
and we know the terrible dimensions of the tragedy.
Yet innocence bears its witness,
that the birds are singing much more than history's Hitlers can sanction,
much more than Darwin allows.

The extravagance of nature lures us,
    woos us into its playtime.
I play with the waves of the ocean, and they play with me.
I play with sounds, words, colors, and I become their playmate.
I play with children, and meet my own forgotten child.
  It becomes a mutual, loving, transforming game.
   It's not so strange; it is redeemed, and I am,
       as I learn to play.

WORKING

This is a tough, but necessary transition.
And sometimes I could be totally persuaded, Protestant work ethic aside,
by Robert Louis Stevenson's "Apology for Idlers,"

to live a life of indolence.

Most of us, however, get acquainted with the fact,

in the land East of Eden where we live,

that there is a connection between working and eating.

Back there in the garden, the animals were named.

But our own animal appetites still clamor to be identified,

and to be fed. Effort's required for that.

The famous eighteenth-century Zen master and painter Hakuin

verified that simple insight with the words

"A day without work is a day without eating."

So life in a Zen monastery is not a continual round of sitting,

avoiding the tasks to which all of us are subject,

and from which we may learn so much.

The alternating and integrated rhythms of turning aside for meditation,

then immersing in activities which make the Zen center run,

are the pattern that we characteristically observe.

How else do we interpret two capping phrases (similar to *koans*)

by Daito, founder of the enormously influential Daitokuji monastery in Kyoto,

"If you hear it incorrectly, you will mistake a bell for a cooking pot,"

and, "Inside the pot, heaven and earth keep a different calendar."

The pot and bell are both validated,

the spiritual and secular timetables are both affirmed.

We are back to *kairos*, intuiting the timing of our tasks,

not choosing between their worth,

and relegating one to a higher, the other to a lower, level of meaning.

Just as, by Frederick Franck's insight,

"A dandelion is in no way inferior to an orchid,"

so Zen democratizes our world,

de-pedestaling some objects and activities

to draw our attention to others.

Mundane chores become luminous with meaning.

Think of the job around your house that you most resent:

it's boring, or unpleasant, maybe you even hate it.

But someone, often you, has to do it.

How do you deal with that?

You might say, "I have better things to do,"

or "Somebody else can do it."

Your ego's pretty visible here.

When you replay those words, conscientiously, are you saying,

"*I'm* better than that job," or "*I'm* better than that person"?

So, if it's your turn, if you really do have to do it,

you whip through it, carelessly,

eager to get on to what's really important.

The Zen center or style may become a health spa for ego-reduction.

The unwanted task gives you a chance to submerge yourself in the task itself

by identifying profoundly with it,

focusing, *mindfully,* on what you are doing,

so that each step is done in full conscious awareness.

"i am *sweeping,*" "i am *washing the dishes,*" "i am *mowing the grass,*"

"i am *changing the diaper,*" "i am *ironing,*" "i am *making the beds.*"

You are the activity.

Savor what your senses tell you in each facet of that job.

Robert Fulghum, author of *All I Really Need to Know I Learned in Kindergarten,*

has a scene in a video, *Everyday Spirituality,*

in which he demonstrates and discusses

how he irons a shirt.

Identify with him, in discovering

a Zen-like quality in the activity.

Smell the fabric of the shirt that you're ironing as the steam rises from it.

Feel the texture of the warm material,

smoothing it carefully before pressing it again.

Hold it up by the shoulders when you've finished,

admiring the completed product.

It's given you a gift.

If you've been aware of the subtle impressions

that have come to you in the process,

then it's told you, through your senses, that you're alive.

Your hands, your arms, your mind, have been there, not somewhere else

in another preferred, fantasized place.

You've been focused on that moment,

and the pure possibilities resident within it.

"You must be present to win."

That's the Zen insight.

Ironing, as an art form??

It qualifies, and you do, as an artist,

if you bring your full attention to that activity,

and many another.

Each chore shares its life with you.

The art of the *do* patterns in Japan, previously mentioned,

lies precisely in their *artless* performance,

in which one is centered, in Nolan Jacobson's words,

"in the deep supportive energies of life,
undisturbed by ulterior motives,
self-conscious focus on technique,
or pre-occupation with some particular style or routine."

Calligraphy may escape the casual Western observer as a bona fide art form.
But catch the subtlety in the simple assertion
"Black ink has five colors."
Is there any way that I can bring that quality of awareness
to the simple tasks I do each day,
discerning the shades of difference, of meaning,
that mark off each moment as unique, pregnant with possibility?
It's intensity of life, not duration of days,
that measures our humanness.
Methuselah, for all his reputed 969 years,
may have been an ephemerid.

Two years ago, one day apart, I participated in memorial services
for two men, ages nineteen and sixty-nine, fifty years apart.
Each was a life of very evident quality.
For Gene Doyle, a student of Zen with me,
the memorial theme might have been
"To an athlete dying young."
For Charles Coolidge, a beloved professor of history,
the mood seemed "Goodbye, Mr. Chips."
Both, with their lives, gave a consummate answer to the confounding challenge
from Robert Pirsig's *Zen and the Art of Motorcycle Maintenance*,
"Define quality."
And very recently, on Valentine's Day 2001,

My friend Francis Ormiston, mentioned earlier
for his vigorous way of arising,
died of lymphoma.
On that day, we simply remembered
That his rich life was a Valentine
gift to us all.
How can I find that same measure of quality,
as these persons have shown it,
in the work that I do, the life that I live?

John Ruskin gave himself the challenge
with the single word *Today* engraved on a stone on his desk.
Would that do it? Refine it still further.
Recall the image of the digital watch.
I would submit that it's a Buddhist timepiece,
which says even more than *Today;*
It says, even shouts,
in the imperious, thunderous voice of the Zen master,
NOW!!

It's the implicit response to many a *koan*, demanding immediacy.
Now is a time word that speaks of quality, not quantity.
NOW is the *kairos*, the timeliness of my time.
If you can invest that quality of *Nowness* into your life, your work,
you have redeemed it.

What am I looking for in Zen, then? What do I expect to find?
Perhaps I am like the Hassidic rabbi who said,
"I did not go to my master to learn his words of wisdom,

but to see how he tied and untied his shoes."
Zen shows up in the artfulness of the ordinary
as well as in the economy of movement of the artisan,
the care of the craftsperson, the patience of the gardener.
Is it possible, in your primary occupation,
and in all the other tasks that you do, with great regularity,
to work in this spirit?
Is that only a romantic ideal? Do you feel victimized by your vocation?
Are you stuck in a dead-end job? Experiencing burnout?
Or do you genuinely enjoy what you do?
Someone has suggested that if you're unhappy in your work,
you're making a dying, not a living.
What's possible? Change of job? Change of attitude?

Some years ago a story seemed to make the rounds of many pulpits.
Preachers liked to tell it.
It told of a man, a curious tourist, who was walking down a country lane
in Europe, where he came to a stone quarry.
In turn, he asked three men what they were doing.
The first gave the obvious answer, "I'm getting this stone out of the ground."
The second gave the practical response, "I'm earning a living."
And the third (at this point the preacher would get a gleam in his eye,
like that of the workman, and with a beatific voice echoed the workman's reply),
"I'm building a great cathedral."

I would suggest that few persons could authentically respond in that fashion.
For the vast majority in today's workforce, the second would be truer:
"I'm earning a living."

In the summer following my graduation from college
I worked as a spray painter's helper in a Boeing plant in Wichita.
My job was to spread "gook" on the bolt-holes of the wings of B-47 bombers,
and when the gook had dried, to shave it off, look for tiny pin-holes,
re-gook it, and shave it once more, till the surface was smooth.
Simple enough. But if the curious traveler from the stone quarry
had come by my work station and asked what I was doing,
I doubt that I would have responded,
"I'm building the arsenal of democracy."
Quite clearly I was earning a living, saving, in my case,
to go to seminary in the fall.
There was little idealism in the job itself, and it was temporary.
But for most on that assembly line there was no cushion
of knowing that you wouldn't be there in a few weeks.
You endured the boredom, the drudgery, because of the wage that you received,
which enabled you to live your real life, apart from your work.
Is that the reality of many situations?

E. F. Schumacher once wrote that the Buddhist point of view
regards the function of work as threefold:
to give the worker a chance to utilize and develop his/her faculties,
to enable that person to overcome ego-centeredness
by joining with others in a common task,
and to bring forth goods and services necessary for a humane existence.

Noble ideals. See if they describe your work setting.
It would be wonderful to see those more commonly practiced.
But most jobs, like mine in the airplane plant,
wouldn't fully measure up. So what do you do?

for work

I am convinced that the best antidote to boredom
is not escape, but attention.
If the situation cannot be profitably changed,
then immerse yourself in it.
Bring an artisan's spirit to your work,
taking pride in your best, most focused effort.

Kuang-ming Wu, in his seminal discussion of play,
elaborated in *The Butterfly as Companion,*
lets us hear the child's voice, which you may recall:
"Nothing to do; (so) no fun."
A child's play is curious, creative; the activity of a budding scientist,
a natural investigator, exploring the world.
If your work doesn't quite fill you with a child's sense of startle and wonder,
if it doesn't always seem like fun,
you do have tasks to perform that may bring you satisfaction.
And if you can't quite, like Snow White's dwarfs,
"Whistle while you work,"
you may at least find some measure of joy,
so that the two realms, *playing* and *working,*
come a little closer together.
And each is equally charming, seductive, intense,
contagious, enjoyable, fulfilling.
Fun, huh? That's Zen.

VII.
CARING AND LOVING

Zen can help us to play and work joyfully, mindfully.
It can also help us to live *heartfully*, in caring and loving.

CARING

I'd like you to meet Kin.
It's unlikely that you'd come across him otherwise,
living as he does in a treehouse, back in a valley
on the Big Island, Hawaii, in a place he calls "Homecoming."
We were lucky to meet him ourselves, on one of his monthly forays
into the small village to supplement
what he can grow for food on his sub-acre of land.

We'd seen him in the village, singular by his "gone-native" appearance,
tall, slender, barefoot, with long hair and beard,
straw-woven hat and skirt, chest covered with palm bark,
carrying a bag of groceries.
Not easy to miss.
My thought: "I'll bet he has a story."

We fell in with him on the steep trail down into the valley,
said hello, introduced ourselves, and heard his name,
repeating it back: "Ken?" "No, Kin, like in kindred, or kinship."
And as we descended the trail, we learned something
of who he was:
his given name the seventh in an English lineage,
a brief stint at Oxford,
a degree from an American university in science,
a lucrative job in industry, then illness, then introspection,
followed by a gradual dropping out,
till he arrived two years ago at Homecoming.
He lives minimally now, in close intimacy with nature,
a solitary, spiritual monastic,
but kin, by his vision, to all.
We walked down to the black sand beach with him,
shared our lunch in a sheltered, idyllic spot,
lingered over good conversation, and parted company,
not having time, regretfully, to join him at Homecoming,
but with many residual reflections.
Time out of time.

I was left recalling a scene at the Art Institute in Chicago years earlier,
where I was standing a little way back from a painting by Paul Gauguin,
a tranquil, South Sea island scene,
with a mother and her small son in front of me,
closer to the canvas.
The child wanted to be anywhere but there,
and was tugging at his mother's arm, eager to leave.
Finally she gave up, and impatiently marched out of the gallery, her son in tow.
I moved closer to the painting and saw for the first time its title,
"Why are you angry?"

There's something about settings like those
that asks questions of our arrived, civilized lives.
Lingering memory traces, maybe, of a garden home,
with limitless implications.
We have our private intimacies, our small social circles,
the work that we do, all the trappings of culture,
and more. But sometimes it may feel like we've been severed
from a wider circle of belonging.
Civilization does indeed breed its discontents.
Weaned too soon, too completely, from the nurturant milk of nature itself,
we may forge desperate, but only pacifying, intimacies
that pass for love, but leave us longing for a true homecoming.
What's missing?
The Zen insight, from Master Dogen, is this:
"To be enlightened is to be intimate with all things."
How can you do that? Doesn't intimacy mean a close, personal relationship

with a family, a few friends? It means a small, shared space,
doesn't it, and regular, tender exchanges with a very limited number of people?
What would it be like to be "intimate with all things"?
Well, maybe that would indeed be an *enlightened* state, and maybe
our needing to ask the question betrays our distance from that condition!
Who are our teachers here? Who can give us those luminous moments
that graduate into life-altering insights?
Perhaps the creatures themselves, the myriad life-forms
that breathe with us, and even the insensate objects of creation.
These, all and each of these, may be vehicles to illumination, enlightenment.

A word of caution to park visitors in the Canadian Rockies counsels us
to keep three bus-lengths of distance from wildlife.
I think that they mean large wildlife, like elk, bears, wolves,
and I see the wisdom in that. You can get too close,
or be part of a dangerous "bear jam" on the highway, trying for photo-ops.
But I think that I can risk getting closer than three bus-lengths
to a chipmunk or a ground squirrel!
I want to get closer, and you do.
That's why we visit national parks, but our presence creates problems.
Maybe we're curious, more than caring.
We're not malevolent; most of us aren't great white hunters,
wanting to bag trophies for our dens, or needing venison.
But we're crowding our forest cousins, and our presence requires management.

A governor of a northern state, some years ago,
wanting to justify an expanded hunting policy on wolves,
made the classic statement, "We can't just let nature run wild out there."

But we know the story of vanishing buffalo herds, and with them
the vanishing of a way of life for Native Americans.
Our presence, in so many ways, has been intrusive, a careless tampering
with nature's delicate balance. It's we who have run wild,
we who require management.

In my first visit to Japan, twenty years ago,
I was sitting on the front porch of an old hotel, almost in the shadow of Mt. Fuji.
It was past climbing season, and Fuji's flanks were veiled in dripping clouds.
Meditative moments for me, leafing through Lafcadio Hearn's
Gleanings in Buddha Fields.
You may recall an image like the one that came to me in these lines:
"In soft rain,
bubbles, in puddles,
explode into life,
then death.
Touch gently."
Life, by Buddhist insight, and our common awareness, is so very fleeting:
One raindrop creates a bubble; the next destroys it.
Given this ephemeral quality, nature's fragile web
in which we are ourselves enmeshed,
all sensitive persons will want to cultivate a gentle, caring spirit.
You do this by remembering in your musings, your meditations,
the myriad creatures of the earth that share this space with you.

Even before he started school, Albert Schweitzer tells us,
he found it incomprehensible that he should pray for humans only
in his evening prayers.

Accordingly, he added his own prayer for all living creatures:
"O, Heavenly Father, protect all things that have breath;
guard them from all evil, and let them sleep in peace."
Much later, living in the jungle which became his place of mission,
making his way with others through a herd of hippopotamuses,
a thought came unbidden: "Reverence for life."
It was the key that opened the door to the rest of his life's reflections,
and to the conclusion, "A man is ethical only when life, as such,
is sacred to him, that of plants and animals as that of his fellow men,
and when he devotes himself helpfully to all life that is in need of help."

In his active life, then, and in his supplications,
Schweitzer joined in a chorus of concern
with Buddhists, Native Americans, and others
on behalf of the four-leggeds as well as the two-leggeds,
the many-leggeds, those who crawl upon the earth,
those who burrow beneath, those rooted within,
those who move through the waters,
those who fly through the sky.
In our vocation of caring, our attentions, our labors
must be devoted to these, and more.

In Japan, perhaps motivated by Buddhist and Taoist sensibilities,
a large group of seamstresses has an intriguing custom.
Once each year they go to a temple, carrying with them
their bent and broken needles—
tools that have served them faithfully in the practice of their craft.
There they immerse them, tenderly, in a large block of tofu,

to the accompaniment of chanting and the wafting of incense.
It is a sacred ceremony,
concluding with the ritual burial of the block of tofu
in a caring farewell to these treasured objects.

How far do you go with this? They're just *things,* aren't they?
But maybe you've driven a car for some years,
and when it seems time to trade it in, you feel disloyal;
you're parting with a friend.
Or give yourself the exercise of clearing out a drawer
that's so stuffed that you can scarcely open it.
Some things you can readily throw away; they were put away mindlessly,
they're readily consigned to the wastebasket.
A few things you keep; you still need or want them.
And now it gets difficult; this requires discipline.
Some objects you hold for a moment, and part with reluctantly, almost reverently.
You have associations with them; they've been part of your life,
but you can't keep everything; you really need to simplify.
Can you identify in some way with the seamstresses in Japan?
There's a Zen mindfulness here.

What would it be like to live in an economy of cherished things,
instead of our own, where worn-out items that have been of worth to us
are thrown out carelessly with the daily disposables,
where fashion dictates a mindless seasonal restyling
and we are subjected to what Murray Bookchin has called
"an engineered pollution of taste by the mass media"?
Perhaps it might instead, as he suggests, awaken in us

"a sense of tradition, with a feeling of wonder
for the personality and artistry of dead generations."
It might mean, also, a simpler, less cluttered life.
Imagine it.
The furnishings in our homes, the tools that we employ,
the garments that we wear, reduced in number, enhanced in worth,
each one, by its utility or artistry,
not simply cluttering our closets,
and crowding all other living space.
Imagine, also, instead of buying and hoarding,
a life guided by making and giving,
freely sharing what life has given to you,
to those who occupy your widening circle of affection.
The objects that you give have been carefully selected, or better still,
you've put up that jar of jam, you've done that handwork,
or made that elegantly simple greeting card?
It holds your personal impress.

Is this something of what caring means?
Its base is expansive, its imagination is almost infinite.
It is expressed in homespun acts of kindness,
in giving directly to noble causes through active involvement,
and through giving of substance with as full as possible engagement of feeling
with those who receive, not in a detached manner, salving one's conscience.
It does not resent the demands of the poor and powerless;
it rejoices in its capacity to respond in generosity of spirit
in whatever ways are open.
If we have developed this capacity, we have provided a wide base of caring
that enables us genuinely to be capable of . . .

LOVING

There's a lot of confusion about the meaning of love.
Sample a few definitions with me—like this one:
"Love is a feeling you feel when you feel you're going to feel
a feeling you never felt before."
Well, that conveys the idea of novelty, and locates love,
clearly enough, in the realm of the feelings,
where it at least partially belongs. Or try this one:
"Life is one thing after another;
Love is two things after each other."
That sort of diminishes the romantic ideal, doesn't it?
But this one puts it back, with syrup:
"Love is two hearts beating as one amid stardust."
Beyond the accompaniment of magic violins, the moonlight and magnolias,
"What is this thing called love?"
Of all life's joys, this one may embrace our highest longings,
contain our highest expectations,

and give rise to our greatest disillusionments.
"It began with such ecstatic excitement, such rich promise,
what went wrong?"
If there is disillusion, there must have been illusion.
If it's founded on fantasy, or a pedestal vision of the other,
it's hard to sustain the illusion in the reality of daily living,
or to modify it gracefully, making necessary adjustments.
That would take discipline, a quality missing in many relationships.
"Love is the strength of disciplined devotion." That sounds better.
It recognizes differences, and covenants to a work ethic within the love bond.

In a classic Zen tale, the questioner asks the master,
"What is the fundamental meaning of Buddhism?"
The master invites him to come outside, and says,
"Look over here: this bamboo is tall, and that bamboo is short."
So in a healthy relationship, one is not better than the other;
the two are simply different.
They are not vying for supremacy or control in a power struggle.
Each values the personal background of the other,
the skills, the tastes, the sensitivities
that the partner brings to the relationship.

If children are part of the equation, the adventure deepens,
as does the challenge!
How very few relationships really prosper
in the face of all the disintegrating forces that operate
within the family, and that bear upon it from the outside!
Each family is set in a context that may nurture or damage;

it is not a self-contained unit.
But a song from earlier in this century perpetrated the fantasy
of self-sufficiency in these lines:

"We'll build our sweet little nest way out in the west,
and let the rest of the world go by."
That's a fiction headed for disaster.
It omits the larger dimension of caring.
Two oysters in one shell begin to cannibalize each other.

Perhaps, despite some very real overlaps,
we can suggest a shade of difference between caring and loving.
For my purposes here, *caring* is the wider term
that links us to all other life and matter,
that gives rise to ecological wisdom, and generates respect
for peoples and their life-styles, values, and belief systems
at great variance from our own.
In our increasingly crowded planet, with both nation states
and plant and animal species vying for limited resources,
we have to care for each other.
To be genuinely human means that we cannot pursue our separate peace.
Loving better describes face-to-face relationships,
where conscious reciprocal exchange is possible.
It describes primary ties between couples, family members, close friends.
Caring and loving impose contrasting challenges and opportunities.
I *care* for my colleagues and co-workers, my students;
The word *love* doesn't quite apply; that's reserved for a smaller circle.
I care about the well-being of a vast range of people

and other possible subjects of concern,
and expect to express that as best I am able.
But distance and finiteness limit that expression.
My circle of love should be expansive,
but that breadth should not threaten the depth of love within it.

It's time for another Zen story, or *koan*.
A questioner appears before the Zen master, and asks,
"What, after all, is the profound meaning of Zen?"
The master replies, "Confucius said, 'I conceal nothing from you.'
Zen doesn't hide anything from you either."
The questioner confesses, as we might, "I don't get it,"
whereupon the master invites him to come with him to a place nearby.
Reaching it, the master asks, "Can you smell the sweet Osmanthus?"
And then he says, "See, I'm not hiding anything from you either."

Maybe the story's not so cryptic.
Zen's intent is to heighten our awareness
of those special gifts which life offers, lavishly, and to share them.
And that's also the intent of love.
Things great and small happen to you in the course of a given day.
Is there a person, or are there a few persons,
with whom you really enjoy sharing these,
and listening to their own stories?
Then there is a quality of love between you.
By contrast, if you are physically close to someone, your partner,
children, family members, and the desire to share is limited,
then you have some work to do.

Communication may be blocked;
you may feel that the other person isn't really interested, or you aren't.
The Zen master said that he was hiding nothing, but you or I may be!
And if we're not actually hiding, there may still be
too many private areas, too many spheres segregated from real sharing.
Examine your close relationships; is there a genuine openness
about acknowledging failures as well as successes,
doubts and fears as well as desires and ideas—
a deep sharing, not just your daily, personal CNN news?
Or sometimes you or I may simply be too lazy for that kind of exchange,
and that laziness takes something away from a real love bond.

How very important love is to us.
The strongest affirmation I ever read of that fact is by Sylvia Ashton-Warner,
a teacher of Maori children in her native New Zealand.
She once wrote in her diary, "I couldn't breathe without love in the air.
I'd choke. I ceased to exist when not in love."
And then she makes the amazing acknowledgment:
"I can quite truthfully say that I never lifted a hand unless *for* someone;
never took up a brush or pen, a sheet of music or a spade,
never pursued a thought without the motivation
of trying to make someone love me."
There's a strange, impossible compulsion in that,
but it does speak of the centrality of love.
Is love, then, the universal creative muse?
William Faulkner, once termed "the grim chronicler of the South's decay,"
claimed the same motivation, saying that he wrote to impress the women he loved.
Whatever he wrote, on whatever theme, however manipulative this sounds,

love was the reason for writing.
Is that a primary motivation for what you do?
And can you drop the manipulation;
simply enabling the other person to grow,
whether or not that person grows toward you?

Another diarist, Sei Shonagon, writing in Japan a thousand years ago,
made love her specific subject matter, not just her inspiration,
describing in *The Pillow Book* her own amours,
and love etiquette and aesthetics.
She celebrates the seasons of love in sensuous detail.
When lovers are together in the summer, she observes,
"It is delightful to have the shutters open,
so that the cool air comes in and one can see into the garden.
But it is pleasant, too, on very cold nights to lie with one's lover,
buried under a great pile of bed-clothes."
You know about that. Not much has changed in a thousand years.
Zen, which helps us in so many ways to celebrate the natural,
helps here to provide a climate for natural, sensuous love:
Zen and the art of cuddling.

Perhaps that's why we see figures called *dosojin*, wayside gods,
at intersections and along roads in rural Japan.
These are not idealized images of transcendent deities;
they mirror human qualities, and some are visibly interested in procreation!
Japan, then, doubtless influenced by Zen, gives abundant validation
to the specifically sexual as well as the broadly sensual.

And the parent-child bond must be celebrated.

Another woman diarist, Frances Karlen Santamaria, asks:

"Why isn't more said about the sensuousness between mother and baby?

It is more than a fringe benefit.

His waking hours infuse my life with a steady sensuous pleasure.

The growing mutual familiarity, the sensations I get each time I pick him up,

the good feeling I get of his heft, his smell . . . and the feel of him—

we merge into one another giving and taking heat, comfort, love."

Many of you, as mothers, will have known that blessing.

Love finds sexual and sensual expression in rich and meaningful ways.

Moving on to friendship,

yet another variety of love, there's so much to affirm.

Whom do you number among your close friends? And how do you define *close*?

These aren't the people to whom you refer when you clarify a relationship

that might have seemed romantic by saying,

"Oh, we're just friends."

The "just" would diminish the bond that you feel.

It would be better to say, "Oh, we're *such* good friends,"

and let them guess!

Sometimes it might almost seem "better than lovers,"

by the quality of its trust, affection, and durability.

I've known such a friend, Shirley Forrer, from a church youth group,

in high school days, who keeps in touch so well with so many people

from those long ago, once-upon days.

It must take time. But when I asked her about that a few years ago,

she said, "I don't lose my friends."

What a wonderful resolution.

Most of us have had friends who,
given our increasing mobility
(and this is one of the casualties of *moving* disproportionately to *staying*),
have passed out of our lives.
When people, who for the claims of friendship-love, do keep in touch,
across the threats of time and distance, the rewards are great.
They've kept intact the most visible threads of life continuity.
Does this thought nudge you to write a letter?

I marvel, too, at the strength of cross-generational friendships.
Marianne, my illustrator, along with a progress report on her drawings,
recounted in an e-mail one of her week's activities:
"Today I took a friend (92 years) to have an eye operation—cataracts—
to be dealt with by laser. She was amazing,
joking with the surgeon as the procedure took place under local anaesthetic.
Tomorrow I'll spend the night with her after she leaves the hospital."
A very simple statement, but eloquent in its descriptive force.
A love bond, clearly. Caring, too, but the full reciprocity is there:
the elderly patient had something to give to her friend and to the physician.

If cross-generational friendships are important,
how much we still need to nurture our ties with our parents.
A Zen story relates how a young man left home
to study with a famous Zen teacher.
On his journey he met a man who asked the youth where he was headed.
The young man repeated his intention.
The other man advised, "Instead of looking for a mere teacher,
you'd be better off looking for the Buddha."

"Do you know where I can find him?" the young man asked.
"When you return home," he was told, "a person wearing a blanket
and with shoes on the wrong feet will come to greet you.
That person is the Buddha."
The youth arrived home late at night. In her joyful haste to greet her son,
his mother threw on a blanket and accidentally put her shoes on the wrong feet.
The son took one look at her and was suddenly enlightened.
Our love ties may provide us with our richest lode—
maybe the mother lode—of enlightenment.

The same can happen between siblings.
If Oedipal dynamics operate in parent-child ties,
another kind of rivalry often dominates
ties between brothers and sisters, as these are complicated by
variables such as birth order,
differences in abilities and temperaments,
and real or assumed favored or non-favored status with parents.
Sibling love takes the same kind of cultivation
as do other family ties.

Two years ago I saw a listing in an Elderhostel catalog that tempted me.
I signed up, and immediately called my brother in Denver:
"Jack, I've signed up for this Elderhostel program in July in western Colorado;
it's called 'Peaks, Poets and Pokes.' "
I described it to him, and asked, "Would that interest you?
I'd love to have you join me."
He said, "That sounds fascinating; why don't you fax me something."
The next day he called and said, "It's a done deal." He'd signed up, too.

We had a marvelous time, with a great group of people,
side trips to colorful places, hikes, guest cowboy poets and singers,
and all the rich lore of that particular region of the American West.
It was the most time we'd spent together since college days,
and we couldn't have had more fun. We've built on that.
Maybe we've tried to measure up to what I've seen my wife and her three sisters,
with their parents, do with their incredible family maintenance skills.

There's a group called The Lead Pencil Club that resists
some of our communication shortcuts,
and stresses personal letters and cards,
birthday and anniversary remembrances,
things that take time but are still some of love's best messengers.
Think of how better attention to words and errands like these
may enrich all of your love bonds.

We usually associate Zen with what seems a stern and solitary practice.
But it was spawned on Buddhist soil, which enumerates among the "perfections"
the quality of loving-kindness.
That also must be part of your Zen informed life.

VIII.

THRIVING AND SURVIVING

Caring and loving, and all the rest have their seasons, their ebbs and flows.
At high tide, we thrive; at low, it is a struggle merely to survive.
But recognizing the seasons, and the need for a durable love
that weathers each, many marriage ceremonies have lines such as
"In health and in sickness, in prosperity and adversity."
Every person needs to maintain some sense of identity
in the face of changing fortunes, and every love bond must also.
Not just for the good times,
but when the going gets rough,
when strains develop, when difficulties tear at your shared fabric,
still, the pledge to make it work.
There are agencies and resources to help. Among these,
religion, in many of its forms,
can enhance the high moments, through celebrative experience.
It can provide coping strategies, problem-solving activity, for the dark days.
Zen, specifically, by its meditative and mindful approach to all spheres of life,
may help us deal with changing circumstances in artful fashion.

THRIVING

No one looks for self-help books
when he or she is riding the crest of the wave.
No one writes them then, either.
Imagine the titles, *When Good Things Happen to Bad People*
or *You're On a Roll!*
You might conceivably buy a copy of the former
for your not-so-good friend who's just won the lottery,
and send it anonymously.
But if you've won the jackpot yourself, you're not in the market.
This isn't the time when most people raise "Why me?" questions.
Maybe, at some level, it should be.
Winning could be a time for ego-inflation, or for careless squandering
or selfish hoarding of the resources that you've acquired.
And sobering reflections such as "Pride goeth before a fall"

might put prosperity in balance; it doesn't always last.

We don't always wear it well while it does, either.

When Joseph in the Biblical record shared his bombastic dreams with his brothers,

he may have come across as an obnoxious, puffed-up pouter pigeon.

And pride may have been their problem, too.

Someone has suggested that it's easier to weep with those who weep

than to rejoice with those who rejoice, because of envy.

Think again of your feelings toward your friend who won the lottery.

There's a challenge from another of the Buddhist "perfections"—

to cultivate the quality of "empathetic joy."

Can you really enter into a friend's good fortune, his happiness,

overcoming the temptation to be envious?

And aren't there legitimate occasions for celebrating the good times,

untainted by such wet-blanket counsels as "Watch out for pride,"

or "It won't last"? There must be.

In the West, we've been told that if we live in fidelity to what we've called

the Protestant work ethic, then we may confidently expect to thrive.

The thriving itself is a visible sign that we have been faithful to our "calling."

That's often seemed a little too neat.

The contrasting theological message, that we deserve nothing

of what we gain or attain, doesn't help much, either.

I once read a doctrinal statement that said,

"Man is inclined toward evil, and only evil, and that continually."

Heavy, really heavy. I doubt that you believe it.

I suspect that our operative theology is provided instead by a pop source, McDonalds,

in their familiar commercial that says, "You deserve *a break today!*"

You really might!

Probably you have worked hard, probably you have been generally virtuous,
so when the ball bounces your way, you don't have to be overpowered
with a sense of unworthiness and the impulse to self-flagellation.
From a Buddhist or Hindu perspective,
you may have accumulated a good *karmic* account.
The deeds that you've performed have accrued to your credit.

And isn't there a time for celebration in which all may share,
the rising tide that lifts all boats? We strive, we thrive, together.
Catch the image of the laughing Buddha, with arms upraised, rejoicing!
What's he celebrating?
Something to do with the experience of being human.
He's awakened to the reason.
There's a Zen story that expands on this image.
A certain monk felt that he could purify his practice by living separately,
apart from the monastic community, on a small island
connected to land by a small bridge.
He vowed never to leave the island.
But three of his friends missed him, and paid him a visit.
They had a delightful afternoon together, and when it came time to leave
they were still talking and laughing so riotously
that the monk did not notice that he had just crossed the bridge with his friends
till one of them exclaimed, "Hey! You just broke your vow!"
The ensuing scene is captured on canvas—
all four monks so dissolved in laughter
that they have to hold on to each other to keep from falling into the water.
A matchless moment.
Even the vow, taken in all seriousness,

is not so holy as the celebration of friendship.
The story underscores the playful element in Zen that we spoke of earlier.
Think of the feast days, the festive celebrations
that other religions and societies foster: Oktoberfest,
Fat Tuesday, Mardi Gras, Carnival, Holi (in Hinduism), and so many more:
shared communal moments that give us occasion to rejoice in being alive.
David Rudder, in his captivating 1998 reggae recording "High Mas,"
articulates what Carnival and similar celebrations may be all about:
"In this bacchanal season,
where some men will lose their reason
but most just want to sway and play
and have a little breakaway
as we seek our lost humanity . . .
So carnival day . . . Everybody come and celebrate
Everybody join the celebration
See the ragamuffin congregate
Every sinner join the jubilation."

How can you access that spirit?
Think of your own communal festivals, the joy you felt;
or make the festival still more intimate.

Begin by taking time with a family member to recall treasured memories:
"Do you remember when . . ."
Family vacations, special evenings, adventures in nature,
when things seemed to come together in such dramatic ways.
For me it happened a few years ago that just as we pulled into the driveway
at my son's home in Denver, anticipating seeing my son, his wife,

and my two grandchildren,
we were all struck to see, as vividly as I've ever witnessed,
a double rainbow in the sky to the east.
Family joy doubly enhanced, and redoubled then by nature
with the sight of the majestic mountains to the west.
Nature spoke to the poet, also, when he observed
a rainbow and a cuckoo's song, each validating the other,
inspiring his own exclamation of praise:
"Lord, how rich and great the times are now."
Think of John Denver's "Rocky Mountain High," and your own,
in whatever location your spirit has been lifted, sublimely,
in those most memorable moments that life offers,
which are part of your birthright as a human.

Maybe you remember a camping trip, a strenuous hike
that challenged each of you but gave you a fine sense of achievement.
Perhaps you're recalling a play, a well-crafted movie
that had you and your companion in stitches or suspense,
a sports event, or your own athletic competition,
or attending a high school or college reunion,
giving you a chance for reminiscing with friends, and,
despite their altered appearances (yours, too!), and despite the years,
finding that you still have so much to talk about.
Surprises, too, in meeting people that you somehow missed earlier,
and finding so much quality in the lives of these lately discovered acquaintances.
Or maybe your most treasured memories are of quiet evenings together
by the fireside, or at your family dinner table,
or decorating the Christmas tree.
And you may recall celebrative events at a temple or church,

in which the visible faith community seemed so vibrantly alive,
and the presence of the Divine seemed quite tangible.
Again, count the ways, all the ways in which you've thrived.
You've built a track record of shared experiences
with those most closely around you. Take time to remember, and to celebrate.

In Hawaii, they use the term *blessings*
for the brief showers that frequently fall, even when the sun is shining.
You don't head for shelter, you welcome the light, refreshing rain.
A few of you who share my legacy of "frontier Christianity"
will recall the old hymn "Showers of Blessing."
The tune and the words resonated for me each time a *blessing* would fall,
in the days that we were in the Islands.
We have all received these blessings, and we will again, and yet again—
abundant occasions for rejoicing.

Try still another activity: stroll around your house with your mate,
or another family member, a room at a time, picking up a cherished object,
hearing and telling its story, and then passing on to others.
How did you acquire those objects? Some of these *blessings* will have been discoveries,
in out-of-the-way shops or at yard sales. And many will have been gifts,
things that someone caringly found or lovingly made for you.

I was browsing in a bookshop in the shadow of Trinity Episcopal Church
in Boston several years ago, when I found a used book of hymns
composed by Phillips Brooks, late-nineteenth-century pastor
of Trinity Church, best known to us by his matchless Christmas carol
"O Little Town of Bethlehem."
That book, in that place, would have seemed auspicious enough,

but inside, in the most beautiful, exquisite gold engraving,
was the equally exquisite greeting of the giver herself, a Catholic nun,
to her friend Mary, written almost a century ago.
I wish that I knew the story of their relationship,
and how this gift, which must have been so treasured at the time,
ever managed to leave the household of Mary's heirs.
Maybe something sad there.

I remember two other most cherished objects,
each made and given to me by one of my sons.
One son's gift is outside in the backyard, a five-foot metal windmill,
carefully crafted, complete with rotating fan. It doesn't pump water,
but it's a loving reminder of my boyhood home in that little Kansas town,
a town of windmills.
The other's object is an exercise in symography, a design shaped
by stretching strings or wires around a pattern of nails.
His design is a series of colorful cosmic ellipses on a rustic board,
their shapes implying motion toward a dark center.
The title, "Saturn Descending into the Vortex," is as imaginative as the art itself!
It decorates a wall in my office, and beckons to worlds beyond.
What associations do you have with your own most cherished objects?
Remember these, and share them.
You will be surprised at what your children will remember, someday.

As a boy, I so much enjoyed my father's art of storytelling, the rich tales
of his own boyhood days. He would get so caught up in the telling
of those incredibly funny stories that we would be laughing at him laughing,
as much as at the stories themselves.
And I wondered if I would have stories like that to tell,

and if I could tell them so well. I'm sure even now that I don't have his gift.
But I was amazed at something that one of my sons told me in a recent visit.
He had remembered a story that I had told of a favorite dog,
a part Boston terrier named Tuck that we had for four years,
when I was about five to nine.
Tuck was maybe named for the happy associations of being tucked in,
or for an early comic strip, "Tuck and Cuddles."
He was a wonderful companion in various adventures,
but one in particular stood out.
My brother and a friend, Bill, both two years older than I, and Tuck and I
were hiking in a field north of town when we came over a hill
and saw a herd of cattle and a large bull that saw us
and began rapidly heading our way.
We started running toward the fence, but we weren't going to make it.
But then Tuck started running circles around the bull, nipping at his heels,
till we got to the fence. Then he cut out and joined us, in safety.
And my son told me how his family had just gotten a dog, a Boston terrier, a female,
and one of her names is Tuck. Imagine it.
Over half a century ago—a little dog, lost too soon
when a drunken driver swerved off the road and hit him
where he waited patiently to cross.
A little dog, remembered now by my son and his children,
and symbolically reincarnated, to give life to them.

Your stories, also, will pass on life's gifts to others,
and you will experience your own life thriving in theirs.
"For the good times . . ."
And for the others, when you're simply . . .

SURVIVING

An old Christian hymn helps you to relate to both thriving and surviving.
"When peace, like a river, attendeth my way,
When sorrows, like sea billows roll,
Whatever my lot, Thou hast taught me to say,
'It is well; it is well, with my soul.' "
That last line is repeated, again and again,
with other circumstances detailed,
underscoring the truth of the state of being
which Buddhists would enumerate among the perfections—
the virtue of equanimity. In all conditions of life.

It isn't an easy state to attain.
The water metaphor, the contrast between a calm river and a raging sea, may be useful.

Think of a geological metaphor, also, in which
the tectonic plates beneath our surface landscapes keep shifting.
Lava keeps erupting, unpredictably, from our psychic core
We may not feel so stable as we look.
It's the familiar condition, the universal fear of
no visible means of support.
You've experienced that, and in ways other than financial,
when you've known real losses, and people and other resources
that you'd counted on just weren't there.
It can be devastating.
An accident, a sudden illness has radically intruded into your comfort zone,
and no one knows how much it threatens your sense of identity.
You may receive the loving care, the necessary medical attention,
but these don't quite reach your deepest needs.
The foundations are shaken.
The feeling may be occasioned by a job loss, or a promotion that doesn't go through,
the breakup of a relationship, a death in your family,
the prospect of dependent aging, or of one day, not too far distant,
of your entrance into a nursing home.
That has to be one of the greatest threats for many, maybe even greater
than the threat of your own mortality.
Sometimes several of these things impact you at the same time,
and suddenly you don't know if you're going to make it or not.
Buddhism calls this state *sunyata;* emptiness, or the Void.

At some point its reality is bound to impact each of us.
Your wave ascends, crests, and you ride it gracefully, joyously.
But inevitably it descends into the trough, and you descend,

even from there, into fathomless depths.

Bunyan, in *Pilgrim's Progress*, called it "the Slough of Despond,"

nothing solid beneath you, no lifelines.

But for Buddhism, the Void is simply where we live, who we are,

in a condition of radical uncertainty, instability.

The crutches that other systems provide are rudely kicked from beneath us;

our cosmic comfort cushions, our fantasied futures are removed.

We're left with life's rawest realities.

Again, *This Is It!* No escapes, no exits.

How do you live with that?

We're told, when we're feeling locked into a tight situation,

to let it go, or perhaps with more courage,

to let it come, facing into the wind, meeting it head-on.

And sometimes we hear the counsel of the familiar Beatles song,

to let it be. "Speaking words of wisdom, let it be, let it be."

This is what is. Accept it. That sounds very Zen-like.

And then the assurance comes, "There will be an answer, let it be."

But Zen takes away even the assurance of answers.

Simply let it be. Rest in the riddle.

The Zen monk Daito once said it, tersely:

"No umbrella, getting soaked,

I'll just use the rain as my umbrella."

The trial itself becomes a shelter, as we accept it.

Few characters in fiction are so memorable as Zorba the Greek.

In some ways his creator could be called "Kazantzakis the Buddhist."

I left a study tour I was leading, years ago, to climb on solo pilgrimage

to the highest spot above the city of Heraklion, Crete,

to where Kazantzakis is buried.

There, beneath the rough wooden cross that marks his grave, in Greek,

are his words, which in English translation read,

"No more fears, no more hopes, I am free."

"Well, yes," we might respond, "I get the 'no more fears' part,

but 'no more hopes'? In the dark hours, what do I have but hope?"

The poet Theodore Roethke may present an alternative challenge when he says,

"In a dark time, the eye begins to see."

It doesn't just see a way out, nor just hope for change.

What that eye may begin to grasp is once more captured

in the Buddhist perfection of equanimity.

Again, that's radical acceptance of what is:

Let it be. Use the rain as your umbrella.

It's so hard for us to imagine how anyone could survive

a tragedy such as that which befell Hiroshima.

But from my brief stay there, twenty years ago, I learned so much

from the survivors, chiefly from my host, the Reverend Kyoshi Tanimoto,

prominently featured as one of several *hibakusha,* or A-bomb survivors,

in John Hersey's book *Hiroshima.*

They exemplified so much the capacity for recovering a sense of mission

and the quality that Robert J. Lifton, in *Death in Life: Survivors of Hiroshima,*

speaks of as "psychological non-resistance,"

perhaps not requiring, in the Western rationalist manner, answers

to the tempting but impossible question "Why?"

before beginning to pick up the pieces of horribly shattered lives and go on.

Maybe they could *rest in the riddle,* even in one of such terrible magnitude.

Victories such as these are not cheaply won.
The same must have been true for Victor Frankl, in surviving the Holocaust.
After reading his unforgettable story in *Man's Search for Meaning*,
you are jolted by his own conclusion:
"I have the feeling that somehow, the best of us did not survive."
Hearing him, also, and seeing his own indomitable spirit,
you want to quarrel with that conclusion.
You know, of course, what he meant; the gentle people, those who could not,
by temperament, strive with the others for scarce food when it came,
yielded their places to others. These didn't make it.
By all that we have been taught, these were the best.
But some, like Frankl, called by his experience to a mission,
responded to an innate imperative not dictated by selfless virtue—that which says
THOU SHALT SURVIVE.
And somehow you know that if Frankl and others did, we can.
Frankl's fierce, tenacious strivings, or perhaps the letting go of the *hibakusha*,
flowing, by some triumph of grace, with the stream, enabled him to survive.
My own struggles, however intense they may feel, pale in comparison
with what persons in Hiroshima and in the Holocaust
have endured. Their experience is beyond my imaginings.

But if their struggles, and my own, are survivable,
then each and all of us face yet another common, leveling challenge:
"How to survive your own death?" Can you?
This is the ultimate *koan* that each of us must penetrate.
Many persons are tutored by hope of personal survival
in some realm where all wrongs shall be righted, all suffering healed.
This self that I know here shall stay intact

to inherit rewards such as "Eye hath not seen, neither ear heard."
The vision is wonderfully compelling, perhaps most of all to those
who have suffered the most.
There's really no quarrel with this; compassion, loving-kindness
dictate a profound feeling for what meets the needs of people in need,
an equally profound respect for our varied survival strategies.
No dogma here. But the voicing, perhaps, of an alternate model,
which Buddhism in general and Zen specifically may suggest.
Like the concept of *sunyata* or the formula *Nirvana=Samsara*,
it conveys a "goal-less goal,"
not one of ego-fulfillment but of ego-transcendence.
The Buddha's silence on the subject of an afterlife is compelling:
"These are questions which do not lead to edification.
Work on reducing suffering."
There are immediate tasks that compel our attention, here and now.
The other concerns indicate my attachment, still, to personal craving,
even to the extent that I am obsessed with my need to live forever.
But consider: why does my sausage-encased ego insist that it must live in perpetuity
in this particular package if life itself is to hold any meaning?
Does that seem egocentric, presumptuous, even arrogant?
When Jesus spoke of finding your life by losing it,
is this part of what he meant?
Or as Shunryu Suzuki observed:
"To live in the realm of Buddha nature
means to die as a small being, moment after moment."

Use the wave analogy again. By some incredible miracle,
the vast ocean of time has borne me up to its crest

for this minuscule moment. I look around, revel in all that I see,

feel the spray in my face, elated by the majesty, the enormity of creation,

grateful beyond belief to be alive.

And then, all my days distilled into this one rising instant of supernal awareness,

all my life breaths compressed into one full-swelling of my lungs,

I exhale, in the most complete letting go that I have ever known,

and sink, in certain confidence and trust, into the depths.

The ocean of time and space which has borne me up will receive me now

unto Itself. All the "special" qualities,

the fictional uniqueness of my separate selfhood,

are now dissolved.

It is my truest homecoming.

I survive, then, in the larger sense, precisely as I yield my need to survive,

I thrive, ultimately, as I overcome my striving.

The Zen master Ryoken conveyed in his death poem this image:

"Sixty-six times have these eyes beheld

the changing scene of autumn.

I have said enough about moonlight,

Ask no more.

Only listen to the voice of pines and cedars when no wind stirs."

It is enough.

EPILOGUE

The Zen teacher Wu Tzu once said,
"Talking about Zen all the time
is like looking for fish traces in a dry waterbed."

Put it to work. Play with it.

ACKNOWLEDGMENTS

I have to begin with my students.
If, as Shunryu Suzuki has so wisely identified the Zen mind as a beginner's mind,
then I must gratefully embrace my student status with them,
in four Honors College classes at the University of South Carolina,
and in workshops here, at the Esalen Institute, and elsewhere.
Zen classes and workshops aren't quite traditional classrooms;
We are co-learners, in experiential situations.

Four former Zen students, in particular,
John Galbary, Jack Gerstner, Lisa Robinson, and Sarah Niegsch,
deserve special accolades for the ways in which
they have continued to help present students.

Then, very logically, my University and my colleagues,
for their constant base of support,
and the South Carolina Honors College,
which has given me so much encouragement for experimentation,
and the two splendid women who have taught Zen workshops with me:
Melody Schaper and Meade Andrews.

Next, my friend and primary mentor in Zen matters, Nolan Pliny Jacobson,
long-time student of Buddhism and Japan,

who died just after Christmas in 1987, and who inspired
my first writing on Zen in his memorial volume.

And then my illustrator, Marianne Rankin, sharer in interfaith matters
in England, now a graduate student at Oxford in religion,
who captures so much of the spirit of Zen
from her artistic sensitivities and extensive residency in Asia.

And Kuang-ming Wu, recent kindred spirit,
whose knowledge of Zen, mirrored in his learned volumes,
is vast and boundless, but who still plays with it,
delightfully, like a child.
He has done me the great favor of a very careful and critical review of these pages.

And very certainly, my wife and other intimate family members,
patient of my pursuits of things strange to them,
and indulgent (generally) and grateful (sometimes)
of my uneven attempts to share and live by insights gained.

Numerous friends and acquaintances, also, in interfaith circles,
most notably Marcus and Mary Braybrooke, Edward Bailey and Peter Laurence,
Seshagiri Rao, Kaushal and Arunima Sinha, and Carl Evans,
who have taught me so much by their models
of acceptance and inclusiveness.

Professional colleagues, too, particularly in the Association for Asian Studies,
Southeast Conference, my favorite such gathering,
where a few papers on Zen received good response,

and suggestions were first heard that there might be a book in this.
With a special word of thanks to John Seabury Thomson,
dear friend and old China hand,
in the fond expectation that his spirit will continue to brood over us.

And two warm and intimate groups: a couples book club,
and the New Generation (with me in it?) Class at Shandon United Methodist Church,
and three Unitarian Universalist Fellowships,
in Hilton Head, Myrtle Beach, and Columbia, each of which,
with people in other local faith communities, Christian and otherwise,
have moved far beyond seeing Zen and meditation as things alien and exotic,
embracing them as natural aids to the spiritual life.

All of the above, by their inspiration and receptivity,
and Robin Sumner Asbury, my first publisher;
John Thornton, my agent; and Cate Tynan and Lauren Marino and others
at Broadway Books, all of whom believed in this project,
have convinced me that "Hey, yeah, Zen is portable—and practical."

FOR FURTHER READING

This list is very consciously selective and not exhaustive.
I've tried to include sources cited in the text,
and a few others that have been seminal for me;
but no attempt is made here at a thorough bibliography.
For persons, however, that want to pursue these matters,
some of these may be useful.

Abram, David. *The Spell of the Sensuous.* New York: Pantheon, 1996.

Blyth, R. H. *Zen and Zen Classics.* Compiled by Frederick Franck. New York: Random House, 1978.

Bookchin, Murray. "A Technology for Life." In *Sources,* edited by Theodore Roszak. New York: Harper and Row, 1972.

Campbell, SueEllen. *Bringing the Mountain Home.* Tucson: University of Arizona Press, 1996.

Chung, Tsi Chih. *Zen Speaks.* New York: Doubleday, 1994.

Franck, Frederick. *The Zen of Seeing.* New York: Random House, 1973.

————. *The Awakened Eye.* New York: Alfred A. Knopf, 1979.

Frankl, Victor. *Man's Search for Meaning: An Introduction to Logotherapy.* Boston: Beacon Press, 1962.

French, Hal W. "Zen and the Art of Anything." In *Buddhism and the Emerging World Civilization: Essays in Honor of Nolan Pliny Jacobson,* edited by Ramakrishna Puligandla and David Miller. Carbondale, Ill.: Southern Illinois University Press, 1996.

Hanh, Thich Nhat. *Peace Is Every Step.* New York: Bantam Books, 1991.

Hearn, Lafcadio. *Gleanings in Buddha Fields.* New York: Houghton Mifflin, 1897.

————. *Kwaidan: Stories and Studies of Strange Things.* Tokyo: Charles Tuttle, 1971.

Hiers, Conrad. *Zen and the Comic Spirit.* Philadelphia: Westminster Press, 1973.

Holmes, Stephen W., and Chimyo Horioka. *Zen Art for Meditation.* Tokyo: Charles Tuttle, 1973.

I Never Saw Another Butterfly: Children's Drawings and Poems from Theresienstadt Concentration Camp, 1942–1944. New York: McGraw-Hill, 1964.

Jackson, Phil. *Sacred Hoops: Spiritual Lessons of a Hardwood Warrior.* New York: Hyperion, 1996.

Jacobson, Nolan Pliny. *Buddhism and the Contemporary World: Change and Self-Correction.* Carbondale, Ill.: Southern Illinois University Press, 1983.

Kraft, Kenneth. *Eloquent Zen.* Honolulu: University of Hawaii Press, 1992.

Lifton, Robert J. *Death in Life: Survivors of Hiroshima.* New York: Random House, 1968.

Merton, Thomas, and D. T. Suzuki. *Zen and the Birds of Appetite.* New York: New Directions, 1968.

Mountain, Marian. *The Zen Environment.* New York: Bantam Books, 1983.

Pirsig, Robert. *Zen and the Art of Motorcycle Maintenance.* New York: Bantam Books, 1984.

Roethke, Theodore. "In a Dark Time, the Eye Begins to See." In *Today's Poets,* edited by Chad Walsh. New York: Scribner's, 1964.

Santamaria, Frances Karlen. *Revelations: Diaries of Women,* edited by Mary Jane Moffat and Charlotte Painter. New York: Vintage Books, 1975.

Shibayama, Zenkai. *Zen Comments on the Mumonkan.* New York: New American Library, 1974.

Snyder, Gary. *Mountains and Rivers Without End.* Washington, D.C.: Counterpoint, 1996.

————. *The Practice of the Wild.* San Francisco: North Point Press, 1980.

Stryk, Lucien, et al. *Zen Poems of China and Japan: The Crane's Bill.* New York: Anchor, 1973.

Suzuki, D. T. *Zen and Japanese Culture.* New York: MJF Books, 1959.

Suzuki, Shunryu. *Zen Mind, Beginner's Mind.* New York: Weatherhill, 1970.

Victoria, Brian. *Zen at War.* New York: Weatherhill, 1997.

Watts, Alan. *The Way of Zen.* New York: Vintage, 1957.

Wu, Kuang-ming. *The Butterfly as Companion: Commentary on the First Three Chapters of the Chuang Tzu.* Albany: State University of New York Press, 1992.

FROM THE AUTHOR

By way of origins I'm a very unlikely candidate to write a book on Zen, an Eastern discipline. My early years were spent near Dodge City, Kansas, almost a prototype of the American West. Maybe in adulthood I needed to study Eastern things for psychic balance. As a young teenager we moved to Wichita, which became the center of a burgeoning aircraft industry in the war years. Older relatives were working to build the arsenal of democracy to fight the Japanese. Then, they were the enemy. Later, I knew that I needed to learn from them.

My spiritual legacy was gained from small-town, "frontier" Christianity. We lived just across the street from the Church, a vital center of life in Mullinville, reflecting simple, homespun values that helped us to make it in those dustbowl, depression days. I decided on the ministry at age fifteen, and my path toward that goal was conventional—studying in church-related schools, and serving another small-town church in Kismet, for seven years. There was still a longing, though, for further education; study at Boston University and McMaster University in Canada fostered an evolution into teaching. For the last quarter century, then, I've been a professor instead of a preacher, with Asian religions as my primary subject, and both feet in the classroom, at the University of South Carolina.

My own root-stock, religiously, is still Christianity—however it seems possible to graft insights from other traditions onto that root-stock, enriching, not adulterating the original. The wisdom and disciplines of Zen, in particular, have been rewarding, not just professionally, but in deeply personal ways. One of those ways is through interfaith activity. Studying and learning from other religious traditions makes it natural to promote understanding between them. I've greatly enjoyed such opportunities, first in England in 1975, and later in North America, and locally at home in Columbia.

My hobbies include travel, a logical association with world religions. I've made many trips to Asia, Western Europe, and various ports of call teaching religion courses for the University of Pittsburgh's Semester at Sea program. I've continued to enjoy singing with choral groups since high school days; two highlights have been singing the Verdi *Requiem* in Canterbury Cathedral and the *Messiah* with the Canterbury Choral Society in the Royal Albert Hall. I enjoy following sports, and brought my glove out of retirement last summer to play shortstop for our departmental softball team!

Along the way, three children have enhanced my life. In a second marriage, three stepchildren; followed in the fullness of time by three grandchildren. My wife, Rannie, helps me in many ways, and shares some of my appetite for Eastern spirituality, particularly when she finds it useful to remind me to be mindful.

—*Hal French*

FROM THE ILLUSTRATOR

My origins make me almost as unlikely a candidate to illustrate a book on Zen as Hal's do to his writing one.

I'm half German, half English, which meant I grew up bilingual and restless. As a child I traveled within Europe. As an adult I've wandered the world, living in far-flung places—the jungles of Borneo, Brazil, and the Philippines before settling in Singapore for sixteen years. I've now returned to the U.K.—at least for a while.

I have always been spiritually restless too, exploring different faiths and the lack of any, before returning to a richer understanding of my own Christian roots. Living in multicultural Singapore led me to a pluralist view of religion and my spiritual journey continues through interfaith activities and an interest in religious experience. I have recently completed a master's degree in the Study of Religion at Oxford University.

Although I have always loved drawing, I learned to paint more recently, helped by Chew Choon in Singapore and Waina Cheng in Oxford. Here I've mixed East and West, and enjoyed a little humor too, with the Little Professor replacing the venerable Oriental sage of old. It has been fun to do, and I hope to have complemented the text visually. After all, so much of Zen is beyond words.

—*Marianne Rankin*